God Has Something to Say About That...

A Divine Call to Excel in the Gift of Grace

Danielle Martin Moffett

authorHOUSE®

AuthorHouse™
1663 Liberty Drive, Suite 200
Bloomington, IN 47403
www.authorhouse.com
Phone: 1-800-839-8640

First published by AuthorHouse 1/29/2009

ISBN: 978-1-4389-4562-0 (sc)
ISBN: 978-1-4389-4563-7 (hc)

Printed in the United States of America
Bloomington, Indiana

This book is printed on acid-free paper.

Dedication

This book is dedicated to my grandmother, Edith B. Martin who is my spiritual role model. You have consistently shown our family what it means to love those who are in need. I love you and I thank you for loving God so much that you share His love unashamedly with all who cross your path. You are the mother of my mother, Jeanette Martin, whom I miss dearly. She pushed my sisters, Brianita and Nicole, my brother, Keith and me to realize our dreams and not just look at them from afar. Your gift of raising my mother to be the woman who nurtured me into being the person I am today is priceless.

Acknowledgments

I acknowledge God as the author and finisher of this book. I thank Him for teaching me to trust in Him and to lean not on my own understanding. I thank God for entrusting to me His voice and giving me the open door to share it with the world. I give all credit to God for the words that are printed in this book. I could not even claim in anyway to be the writer of this book; I can only say that I am God's inspired writer. It is God whom deserves the praise and whom should receive the glory and with that I am satisfied.

I want to thank my family for their continuous encouragement and patience during the writing of this book. I thank my husband, Frank Moffett Jr. for seeking God on my behalf and speaking God's truth to me. I also thank him for undergirding God's mission for me and pushing me to be honest with myself and with God. Honey you truly have become for me a loving picture of Christ's grace in my life. Thank you for your love and your support. I love you! To my daughters, Jade and Jordan and my sons Frank 3rd and Daniel: Thank you for the laughs, and your belief in me. I thank God for giving me 4 great gifts. I love you very much and am so proud of you.

I thank God for the many believer's who have sowed in my life and have upheld me during this journey of writing. I thank you all for holding me accountable to God's word, and pushing me to fulfill God's calling. I am very grateful for your love and faithfulness. I especially want to thank my Personal Touch Christ Center Church family and Pastor Diane Cooper; two of my Palmer Theological Seminary Professors, Dr. Ron Sider and Dr. Craig S. Keener for their influential teachings about God's justice and mercy that's required of us all; Apostle Raymond Stansbury and Christine Payne for their unselfish help and last but certainly not least my very supportive sister, Brianita Bishop and sister in Christ Andrea Galloway.

Love,

Danielle Martin Moffett

Foreword

Like a song in a singers voice, and a pen in an author's hand their goes the multitude. It is but the rare one who can light a fire in the hearts and ears of the hearer and in the heart and the mind of the listener. That is you. You are a rare one. A rare one who listens and follows and does what thus says the Lord. It is not I, who I am to please. It is not I, who am to look at the words on the page and be pleased with my words and have the words I write on the page move me. But the words written should move those whom God has ordained to hear, to see and to read. It is not I.

On this day, God revealed the truth hidden in my heart and then with great care and love for me, God overlaid His heart upon mine changing how I would write and think about writing for the rest of my life. God wanted me to know there are many writers and many voices in the earth. There is not a shortage of books and songs on the shelves. There is not a shortage of author's and singers; nor a shortage of those reading and listening to published works. Many judge their singing and their writing by their own heart and it is with their own mind they decide the outcome of their final work. If it feels good and moves the writer then surely it shall move the multitude right? It may, but that is not God's way. God says the writer must be moved by the heart and mind of God alone thus bringing the voice of God on the earth edifying the hearer and the reader. God's writers are to produce writings for God's people to experience change, to be renewed, to be lifted up, to ignite a spark in the mind and the heart kindled by the very truth of God. My hope for the readers of this book is that you will find the greatest treasure on earth through the revealed Word of God that points us to Christ. Praise God for His indescribable gift of Grace!

I pray with all my heart that God's heart is revealed to you.

Danielle

Table of Contents

Isaiah 55:1-3

"Come, all you who are thirsty,

come to the waters;

and you who have no money,

come, buy and eat!

Come, buy wine and milk

without money and without cost.

2 Why spend money on what is not bread,

and your labor on what does not satisfy?

Listen, listen to me, and eat what is good, and

your soul will delight in the richest of fare.

3 Give ear and come to me;

hear me, that your soul may live.

I will make an everlasting covenant with you,

my faithful love promised to David."

Unifying God's People

God has something to say about unifying the Body of Christ. God's commandments, statues and judgments points to one end result, His people unified in thought, word and deed in Christ Jesus. We are to make every effort to keep the unity of the Spirit through the bond of peace. (Ephesians 4:3)

God's economy principles unify His people. God gives us the power to get wealth. Those who agree with God in our faith-walk are those who also receive of God's faith-wealth for the purpose of doing God's faith-works in the earth. We are all expected to do our part to contribute to and help the whole of God's Kingdom economy. Our faith-walk brings to us faith-wealth to perform faith-works. This is true for those who have and those who have not. In God's economy there are those who are wealthy, having overflow large or small and those who are poor, having neither overflow nor enough to meet their basic daily needs. God requires those who have received of His faith-wealth to operate in faith-works by being open-handed and generous, giving to the poor relieving their suffering. Giving to the poor fulfills God's command to have no poor among the people of God. God's command should never be misinterpreted as a suggestion but it should be viewed as a must for the chosen treasured people of God. Yes, we have read in the Bible, both in the old and new testaments, there will always be poor among you. This statement is a call to action for believers to get our brothers and sisters in Christ out of poverty. This statement is not a call to passive observance and acceptance of the existence of poverty in the world. We are not to walk on the other side of the street to avoid our brother and sister who is in need of help. But we are to come into agreement with God and care for the needs of the poor.

God wants His people to act on His word going beyond meditating on it. God has promised life and prosperity to all who follow His commands. The glory of God has been given to us to unify; showing our love for one another and displaying to the world the greatness of our God. Our God is one and we are one in Him. (John 17:20-23)

God Has a One-Mind Focus

- We are to worship and serve one God. (Luke 4:8)

- God chose one man to bring forth the nation of Israel (Hebrews 11:12)

- God is one; Jesus said I and the Father is one. (John 10:30)

- By one sacrifice for sins Jesus Christ has made perfect forever those who are being made holy. (Hebrews 10:12-14)

  o One new creation in Christ; the old has passed away, all things are new (2 Corinthians 5: 17)

  o One new man in Christ; peace between the Jew and Gentile, salvation has come to the Gentile nations also. (Ephesians 2: 14-18)

  o One new covenant; God's laws are written in our hearts and minds, our sins are forgiven and remembered no more, no more sacrifices for sin. (Hebrews 9:15)

- There is one body and one Spirit- just as you were called to one hope when you were called- 5 one Lord, one faith, one baptism; 6 one God and Father of all, who is over all and through all and in all. (Ephesians 4:4-6)

It is through the Unity of faith and knowledge of the Son of God that the body of Christ becomes mature and attains to the whole measure of the fullness of Christ. (Ephesians 4:12-13)

Unity is Oneness

God's desire is for the body of Christ to be bought to complete unity so the world will know that our Father sent the true Messiah Jesus Christ to us. The world will see that our Father loves us just as He has loved our Savior and Redeemer. To ensure that the body of Christ attains to Oneness, Jesus gave us His glory full of Grace and Truth; the same glory that made Jesus one with the Father in heaven while He was on earth. This glory enables all of us who believe in Jesus' message to be one with each other in Christ and one with Jesus. We will be one as Jesus and our Father is one. (John 17:21-23)

Unity in Giving

God, revealed in 2 Corinthians chapter 9, He wanted the Church of Achaia in Corinth to unify in giving to the poor saints in Jerusalem. They already excelled in faith, in speech, in knowledge, in complete earnestness and in their love for the elders of the church. Now it was time for them to also excel in the grace of giving that unifies the wealthy and the poor saints in the Kingdom of God. (2 Corinthians 8:7) God gave the Church at Achaia the power to get wealth. Faith-wealth is not given to His people to store it, to hoard it and to selfishly use it for our own needs alone. Wealth is given by God to believers to confirm His covenant of love to His people. God promised to keep and provide for all who love Him and keep His commandments. It is the wealth God produces that eradicates poverty in the Kingdom of God by re-distributing the wealth to ensure no one has too much and no one has to little. Now that the wealth of God is in the hands of the Church at Achaia will they honor their profession of faith in Christ and do the righteous works of God? Will they give to their brothers and sisters in Christ who are poor and in need of help?

In 2 Corinthians 9 God teaches us He uses seed sowing as a means to unify His people in thought, word and deed. The church at Achaia were from a Gentile nation and the requested collection was for those of the Jewish nation bringing opportunity for the peace Jesus bought to the earth, to prove the unity of the one new man in Christ. Grace is the Force of God that helps us live godly and righteous lives. Love is the tie that binds everything together. Grace is what enables the church at Achaia and you and me to unify the church in giving. With the power of God's love and the force of God's grace, believers are able to unify under the banner of giving and receiving or sowing and reaping, relieving all manner of poverty in the Kingdom of God. This confirms God's truth to keep and care for His covenant people. To each one of us grace has been given as Christ apportioned it. Grace transforms us from being selfish consumers (eating the bread) of our

God given wealth only to being "sowers" also of the faith-wealth seed God has placed in our hands.

The wealth of the Kingdom of God has been placed in the hands of God's Children.

In this book when we speak of hands we are speaking both figuratively and literally. Figuratively like the part of the song, "Joy to the World", which says "He's got the whole world in his hands". The use of the word hands in this song means, God owns and cares for the world; as opposed to the world literally sitting in the palm of his hands. Figuratively speaking in this book, the hands of God's Children mean the people of God care for the faith-wealth resources given to us in God's Kingdom while we are on the earth. We are to care for and rightly use the blessings of the earth and operate faithfully in the spiritual blessings in the heavenly realm. Literally our hands hold the spiritual and physical seed of God. God is the giver of all seed, spiritual, financial, material possessions, knowledge, wisdom, etc. We are responsible to God for sowing the seed he has put in our hands. If the seed is knowledge, share it. If it is financial, sow it. If it is material possessions, give it. Our bodies are to be spiritual sacrifices unto the Lord, we are not our own, we have been bought with a price. Although we have many gifts and talents given us by God that we can sow into this world, this book is primarily focused on the context of 2 Corinthians chapter 9 which speaks to God's children about unifying in and sowing the gift of financial and material seed. God has called me to tell His people the truth about 2 Corinthians chapter 9. God said, "My people reason too much!" The truth of God overcomes excessive reasoning of the mind and unifies the body of Christ in the word of God about giving and receiving.

> 2 Corinthians 9:10-11 "10 Now he who supplies seed to the "sower" and bread for food will also supply and increase your store of seed and will enlarge the harvest of your righteousness. 11 You will be made rich in every way so that you can be generous on every occasion, and through us your generosity will result in thanksgiving to God."

God gives seed to the "sower", and bread to eat. Every believer has seed in their hand. What we do with that seed will determine our future and our ability to contribute to the growth of the Kingdom economy of God. What we choose to do with the seed God gives us is not a matter of our opinion on how seed grows and it's not a matter of our desires, plans or goals for the future. Our seed is to be sown according to God's purpose; the purpose of prospering His word on the earth. God works in you and me to will and to act according to his good purpose for our good and the good of the Kingdom. Sowing seed is a spiritual act of the will first. The fear of the Lord and the wisdom of God guide our sowing.

Philippians 2:12-13 "....continue to work out your salvation with fear and trembling, 13 for it is God who works in you to will and to act according to his good purpose. "

God's desire is to make His children shine like stars on the earth as He works through us His good and mighty purpose. The Lord our God is one. We serve the one and only true and living God. He is God over heaven and earth; everything in it and everyone on it. It is from Him that we have willingly received our Salvation which is full of grace and truth. Our Salvation provides us with the grace of sure safety, rescue, deliverance, protection and provision. Our Salvation also provides us with truth and instruction to carry out God's will and thoughts on earth. The Bible instructs us to not neglect our Salvation. (Hebrews 2:2) We are to work out our Salvation continually with fear and trembling. It's true we can not earn our Salvation. It's also true, once we receive of God's grace of Salvation and its benefits we become apart of a greater Kingdom not made by human hands, wisdom or strength. We become citizens of the great Kingdom of God ruled by our great King Jesus Christ. Under His great banner of righteousness, redemption and wisdom we move and have our being. We live in the earth but our wisdom is not of this world; just as our King is not of this world. Our wisdom teaches us to sow seed differently than the world sows seed. God has given us instructions on how to sow for a perpetual harvest that not only blesses us in the earth, but also blesses us eternally in heaven and increases the growth of the Kingdom of God. God has written His law on our hearts and minds so that we can know Him, understand Him and in knowing God we are willing to follow Him and obey His truth.

Truth comes from one place – heaven. We call truth from heaven – revelation, or the revealed word of God. The revealed word, which was once hidden from us and now uncovered and made known to us, seizes our heart and the truth when practiced, sets us free. (John 8:31) Receiving revelation makes us bold and unashamed to give voice, will and action to the truth in private and public. The ultimate truth revealed from heaven can never be overcome by anyone or anything giving the receiver of revelation a sureness that can not be denied.

Herein is a faith-wealth revelation: It is God who gives us the ability or power to get wealth. (Deuteronomy 8:17, 18) Getting faith-wealth begins with seed. The seed is the Word of God sown into the hearts of men and written on the mind. The seed that's sown in our heart must take root in the field of our heart in order to produce a harvest. We must let the word of God mature in our field by keeping the word in our heart and persevering through times of testing, and life's worries, pleasures and riches. Once the seed matures it is capable of growing and producing a mighty harvest 30, 60 or 100 fold. (Mark 4:2-20) Mature saints in the word of God become productive "sowers" in the Kingdom of God. Productive "sowers" of God, sow in righteousness which is the key to prosperity. Prosperity comes to us when we perform the righteous acts of God such as sowing in the lives of saints who are in lack financially, materially and spiritually. The Kingdom of God is within us. (Luke 17:21) It's the "sowers" seed, the seed of the Word in us that reaps a harvest. We are the "sowers" of God who have received of the mysteries and secrets of the Kingdom and have put them into action on the earth to reap mighty blessing in and for the Kingdom of God. The seed of the word is the source of production. It's the stepping stone into our future.

Seed time and harvest begins with God and ends with God. He's the giver of the seed and the giver of the harvest. When we speak of reaping harvest in this book, it's a harvest that grows because the seed of the word matured first. God has put His seed in our hearts, minds and hands. What are you going to do with your seed?

Deuteronomy 8:17-18

17 You may say to yourself,

"My power and the strength of my hands have produced this wealth

for me."

18 But remember the LORD your God,

for it is he who gives you the ability to produce wealth,

and so confirms his covenant, which he swore to your forefathers, as it

is today.

Matthew 25:14-18   "14Again, it (the Kingdom of Heaven*) will be like a man going on a journey, who called his servants and entrusted his property to them. 15To one he gave five talents of money, to another two talents, and to another one talent, each according to his ability. Then he went on his journey. 16The man who had received the five talents went at once and put his money to work and gained five more. 17So also, the one with the two talents gained two more. 18But the man who had received the one talent went off, dug a hole in the ground and hid his master's money."   (*emphasis added)

The Parable of the Talents in Matthew 25:14-30, expresses God's will for His servants to manage His Kingdom wealth. The Master in this parable chooses which servants he wants to prosper his property. The servants did not choose the Master. The Master gives "seed money" to three of his servants according to their ability to prosper his kingdom. To one servant he gave five talents, to another he gave two talents and the third servant he gave one talent to sow. The more "seed money" they received reflects the Master's belief in the servant's abilities to increase his property. No matter how much money they receive, a little or a lot, what they have in their hand was expected to grow according to the will of the Master. The servants are in the service of the Master. Who will be judged faithful, wise and a good servant at the judgment? Who will be judged unfaithful, foolish and wicked servants?

The Parable of the Talents communicates this key point: how we choose to live our life on earth will determine our eternal rewards or our eternal punishment. Eternal rewards are given when we live our lives in service to God; eternal punishment is given when we live our lives in service to another besides our God. Matthew 25 is sandwiched between, "The signs of the end of the age" in Matthew 24 and "The judgment at the end of the age" in Matthew 26 giving us a clue Matthew 25 is in the same context as judgment and the end of the age. Thereby concluding we will be judged on how we handle God's money and property. The opportunity to be judged faithful in managing God's money and property is laid before each of us. Receiving God's eternal rewards is possible for every believer. God has chosen us and ordained us to bring forth fruit that last. (John 15:16-17) This is to our Fathers' glory that we bear fruit showing ourselves to be Jesus' disciples. (John 15:8) They will know us by our fruit. This fruit abounds to our heavenly account.

Matthew 25:19 "After a long time the master of those servants returned and settled accounts with them."

The servant's Master returned to settle accounts with each servant. The servant with five talents in this parable bought forth a harvest of fruit of five more talents from the seed he was managing. The servant with two talents of money increased his seed by two more talents. They deposited into their fruit accounts double their seed sown. They were judged faithful with a few things and the Master put them in charge of many. He bid them to come unto him and to share in the Master's happiness! The result was he gave them more and he gave them abundance. They were rewarded for their faithfulness in prospering their Master's money. Oh how God longs to have His children rewarded with abundance.

> Matthew 25:20-23   "20The man who had received the five talents brought the other five. 'Master,' he said, 'you entrusted me with five talents. See, I have gained five more.' 21"His master replied, 'Well done, good and faithful servant! You have been faithful with a few things; I will put you in charge of many things. Come and share your master's happiness!' 22"The man with the two talents also came. 'Master,' he said, 'you entrusted me with two talents; see, I have gained two more.' 23"His master replied, 'Well done, good and faithful servant! You have been faithful with a few things; I will put you in charge of many things. Come and share your master's happiness!"

Just like in the Parable, sometime in the future, at the judgment of the Lord, Jesus will settle the accounts of each of His servants. We all must be aware each one of us has an account in heaven. If we don't understand this truth we won't work to make deposits into our accounts.

Matthew 25:24-30   "24 Then the man who had received the one talent came. 'Master,' he said, 'I knew that you are a hard man, harvesting where you have not sown and gathering where you have not scattered seed. 25So I was afraid and went out and hid your talent in the ground. See, here is what belongs to you.' 26"His master replied, 'You wicked, lazy servant! So you knew that I harvest where I have not sown and gather where I have not scattered seed? 27Well then, you should have put my money on deposit with the bankers, so that when I returned I would have received it back with interest. 28" 'Take the talent from him and give it to the one who has the ten talents. 29For everyone who has will be given more, and he will have an abundance. Whoever does not have, even what he has will be taken from him. 30And throw that worthless servant outside, into the darkness, where there will be weeping and gnashing of teeth.'"

The servant with the one talent to sow didn't work to increase his account. He chose not to sow the money but to bury it. When the master came to settle his account the only increase he had was an increase of reasons why he didn't multiply his seed. All too often God's experience with His servants is like this servant. We come up with reasons and excuses as to why we couldn't or wouldn't handle God's money and property according to His will.

"My people reason too much!" says the Lord.

The Master's money was given to this unfaithful servant according to his ability. He was thus graced with the skill to prosper the Master's Kingdom but instead chose to do nothing to increase or grow the property entrusted to him. Fear was his reason and excuse; laziness was the Master's interpretation. Another one of his reasons and excuses was that the Master was a hard man, harvesting where he did not sow and gathering where he did not scatter seed; wickedness was the Master's conclusion. This servant shows us we can know the will of God and know the characteristics of God and still not follow God's instructions. We are responsible for what we know. This servant also shows us we can be given the talent and property of God and hide it or ignore it preferring to focus attention and interest on other things. By "reasoning too much" this servant became unreasonable and did foolishness in the sight of the Master instead of using his abilities to accomplish the Master's will.

God knows our skills and abilities also. He gives us the grace to manage the seed He has given us. God has given us every spiritual blessing in the heavenly realms in Christ Jesus to prosper the seed and to bring forth fruit that abounds to our heavenly account. Anytime we obey God's word we bear good fruit. (John 15:5-10) When we witness Christ to the nations, we bear good fruit. (Romans 15:15-18) When we give to the poor and needy saints we bring forth righteous fruit that last. (2 Corinthians 9: 9-10, Romans 15:25-28) When we sow into the mission of Godly ministries and administrators, our fruit is credited to our heavenly account. (Philippians 4:14-17)

Focus Your attention on Good Fruit that Last

When we bring forth fruit that last it's credited to our accounts, showing us to be disciples of Jesus Christ and bringing glory to the Father. When we bear good fruit, we are doing what Jesus did; we are walking in agreement with Christ and thus following the commands of Christ. When we follow the commands of Jesus Christ we are showing our love to Him and by remaining in Him, God causes us to bear fruit. No one can bear fruit without abiding in Christ and Christ abiding in us. Therefore, the word of God says if we do this, then we can ask for anything and we will have it.

John 14:12-14 "12 I tell you the truth, anyone who has faith in me will do what I have been doing. He will do even greater things than these, because I am going to the Father. 13 And I will do whatever you ask in my name, so that the Son may bring glory to the Father. 14 You may ask me for anything in my name, and I will do it."

John 15:5-8 "5 I am the vine; you are the branches. If a man remains in me and I in him, he will bear much fruit; apart from me you can do nothing. 6 If anyone does not remain in me, he is like a branch that is thrown away and withers; such branches are picked up, thrown into the fire and burned. 7 If you remain in me and my words remain in you, ask whatever you wish, and it will be given you. 8 This is to my Father's glory, that you bear much fruit, showing yourselves to be my disciples."

Bringing forth fruit that last is righteousness in action. God promises when we do acts of righteousness such as giving to the poor, He will reward us and increase the fruits of our righteousness. Our fruit will be plenty and in abundance. God always remembers the work we do and He always repays us for our love, kindness, compassion and obedience.

The word of God is not some kind of magic potion to be used at the whim of anyone who can read it and speak it. The word's power is in the faithful relationship between God's people and God. The servant who follows God's teaching, instructions and commands is blessed with more and in abundance. The servant who chooses not to follow God's instruction, even what he has will be taken away. To those who have been given much, much is required. Those who are faithful over a little will be ruler over much more. Our faithfulness in sowing the seed our Master has entrusted us with or delivered to us will determine our earthly and heavenly rewards.

Matthew 25:29 " For everyone who has will be given more, and he will have an abundance. Whoever does not have, even what he has will be taken from him."

The wicked servant in the parable of the talents was called worthless and thrown out. What he had was taken from him and given to the faithful servant. There was a simple alternative to burying the one talent of seed money. This servant could have at a minimum deposited the money with bankers in order to increase the Master's property. This action would have enabled him to draw interest on his account.

Matthew 25:27 "Well then, you should have put my money on deposit with the bankers, so that when I returned I would have received it back with interest. "

Some increase is better than no increase.

This is a parable with great insight into how God thinks about sowing and reaping. The seed God gives us He makes us ruler over. We must take charge of God's money and property and be accountable for its increase. We are made to be queens and kings over the seed to make decisions that would prosper the Kingdom of God. And if we do nothing else we need to at a minimum give the seed to the bankers and draw a harvest of interest for our Master. This is a very common way of sowing seed today.

We see this Godly principle of sowing and reaping being reflected in the Banking Industry. If you sow your money into an interest bearing account, you will receive a harvest which is a multiple of what you sowed. This original concept of God, seed sowing and seed multiplication (increase or harvest) is copied by the world and the majority of mankind believes in and participates in this seed sowing and seed multiplication through the world's Banking System.

Why then do we so readily embrace, accept and participate in the world's multiplication system but we reason away God's multiplication system?

We settle for the copy and forsake the original even though it's the greater. We have a blind faith in the Banking System. We have a high comfort level with giving our money to the bankers even though, the parable of the talents suggest putting your money into the bank and drawing interest is a way to increase but not the greater way to multiply our seed. Jesus doesn't reject the Banking Industry; He just positions it at the lower level of multiplication. We settle for lower levels when our understanding is at a lower level. But God has positioned us in Christ to understand at a higher level which is a heavenly level.

Investing with World Bankers can provide us a "form" of prosperity, but true prosperity is designed by God. To reach the true level or the highest level of prosperity we must trust in the wealth maker.

Deuteronomy 8:18 "But remember the LORD your God, for it is he who gives you the ability to produce wealth, and so confirms his covenant, which he swore to your forefathers, as it is today."

Therefore our seed sown would be best placed where the seed giver, the wealth maker, God Himself instructs.

As we see in the world everyday there is a level of wealth anyone can gain from sowing financial seed in the world's financial system whether you are a believer in Christ Jesus or not. Believers ought to know how Jesus wants us to obtain our faith-wealth and receive God's prosperity. This is important because even though we live in the world, the Bible says we are citizens of heaven, even aliens living in this world. (John 17:16) Our ways of doing things are not limited anymore by what's available to us through the world. Our prosperity therefore should no longer depend on the worldly copy of gain but we should depend on God to fulfill His will for our lives; His will for our prosperity. In Christ Jesus, we have been set up to receive the highest level of prosperity available to mankind. We know longer are among those who have to settle for less. We can and are able in Christ to operate in the perpetual prosperity of heaven in God's glorious riches found only in Jesus Christ our Lord.

Philippians 4:19 "And my God will meet all your needs according to his glorious riches in Christ Jesus."

To obtain this glorious level of perpetual prosperity we must believe God's Authoritative Word. We must faithfully receive God's Word and confidently trust it will produce the highest level of prosperity toward us who believe. God's will is that our soul prospers in His word. A soul that prospers in God's word brings forth good fruit of good health and prosperity. "Beloved, I wish above all things that thou mayest prosper and be in health, even as thy soul prospereth." (3 John 2, KJV)

God is pulling us up to His desire for us. Won't you receive God's calling?

Romans 8:28-30 "For those God foreknew he also predestined to be conformed to the likeness of his Son, that he might be the firstborn among many brothers. 30 And those he predestined, he also called; those he called, he also justified; those he justified, he also glorified."

For those God predestined, He also called, justified and glorified. God predestined us to be saved before the foundation of the world. God called us to be made in the image and likeness of Christ. He didn't stop there; for many are called but few are chosen (i.e. few choose to walk in what God has called them to do). Whoever receives God's calling of Salvation by faith in Christ, God justifies, enabling through the purified blood of Jesus to qualify as a son of God able to perform the good works of God. Once justified by God we have access to dwell in, participate in and operate in God's glory. We come to live in a glorified state in Christ Jesus our Lord. We become a citizen of heaven and a member of the Kingdom of God. God lifts us up to the highest level of being, the highest level of existence in the world. We are no longer in a kingdom of talk, a copy of light, but we are now in the Kingdom of God which is the Kingdom of Power and of almighty light. Come up to this glorified existence and operate in God's glorious power available and destined by God for us to participate in!

> 2 Peter 1:3-4   "3 His divine power has given us everything we need for life and godliness through our knowledge of him who called us by his own glory and goodness. 4 Through these he has given us his very great and precious promises, so that through them you may participate in the divine nature and escape the corruption in the world caused by evil desires. "

We have been discussing two different vehicles for Seed Sowing, the world's system and God's system. Where we sow our seed will depend on our desired harvest. If our desired harvest is money, then use the world's copy of seed sowing and draw interest and the work is done. We've achieved our goal. We can reap our harvest. On the other hand, if our desire is more and we have a need that money alone can't solve; then we must rise up to God's highest way of seed sowing and multiplying. The prosperity harvest of wholeness, fruitfulness, health, money, peace, joy, wisdom, revelation and much more awaits those who choose God's way by submitting to God's will.

My prayer for every believer is we all submit unto the knowledge of God's truth and reject reasoning that is not in service to God's word. I pray we resist being seduced by the wealth of this world for it is limited and deceitful producing no eternal value or reward. However, consistently and sincerely following God's righteous and faithful way in handling our God given wealth is remembered by God forever producing eternal favor and perpetual prosperity.

> Romans 8:31-33 "What, then, shall we say in response to this? If God is for us, who can be against us? 32 He who did not spare his own Son, but gave him up for us all-how will he not also, along with him, graciously give us all things? "

God is willing and God is able to freely give us all things. He has already given us His ALL in Christ Jesus. There is nothing that is good God wants to withhold from us in Christ. He has already provided for all our need. I hope you are getting this revelation. God has sown his highest level for us, His Son Jesus the Christ, so that we in Christ can rise to the highest level available to mankind. It's "the hi position" God raised mankind to in the beginning at the creation of the world.

> Genesis 1:26-27 "26Then God said, "Let us make man in our image, in our likeness, and let them rule over the fish of the sea and the birds of the air, over the livestock, over all the earth, and over all the creatures that move along the ground." 27 So God created man in his own image, in the image of God he created him; male and female he created them."

God called us to be like Him and He gave us a position of authority and "the hi status" of dominion over all the earth. Mankind lost this high status in Genesis 3 when Adam and Eve allowed Satan to seduce them into reasoning away their dominion and authoritative rights. Satan reasoned with Adam and Eve convincing them that disobeying God's command would bring them to an even higher position of dominion and authority than God had given them. This lie seduced their minds, distorted their perception and caused them to follow Satan and forsake God; lowering their position, status, dominion and authority and of all mankind born after them. The false allure of grandeur promised them by Satan took away the eternal favor and perpetual prosperity from mankind. Mankind started living in the copy of the original between two worlds, the world of good and the world of evil. The twisted deception by Satan to re-interpret God's command saying they would be equal to God if they ate of the forbidden tree made it seem as if this action would catapult man into a higher state of existence but it backfired.

The true result is it took mankind from an intimate, close personal relationship with God where every provision and need was supplied. Mankind didn't have to labor for anything because God freely gave mankind every thing. Instead the act of not following God's way led to mankind being thrown out of privilege living. Afterward man had to labor and toil for food, shelter and clothing. For the first time mankind experienced evil harvest in the world. But God our Father, with great love and compassion for mankind and great mercy in His heart prepared for man a gift of eternal redemption in His Son. Christ, the Savior of the World, was sent to reverse the curse that took away our eternal reward of perpetual prosperity and eternal favor. God sent Jesus our Lord to crush the seed of Satan by His blood sacrifice and the tearing of His flesh at the cross. God's plan to return mankind back to our original "high place" through the death, burial, resurrection and ascension of Jesus the Christ has worked. Victory over Satan has been accomplished in Christ Jesus. For all of us who believe in Jesus Christ, eternal life has been restored and every spiritual blessing in the heavenly realms has been given to us. (Ephesians 1:3) Christ' victory made provision for all mankind to be reconciled to God enabling all who receive of God's gift of Jesus Christ to experience God's glorious riches today through eternity. For God says if I have given my Son for you I will not withhold anything from you.

All things include the wealth of the Kingdom of God in which Christ has already received to give to us also.

Revelation 5:12 "In a loud voice they sang: "Worthy is the Lamb, who was slain, to receive power and wealth and wisdom and strength and honor and glory and praise!"

To God is the glory forever!

Malachi 3:6-12

6 "I the LORD do not change.

So you, O descendants of Jacob, are not destroyed. 7 Ever since the time of your forefathers you have turned away from my decrees and have not kept them. Return to me, and I will return to you," says the LORD Almighty.

"But you ask, 'How are we to return?' 8 "Will a man rob God? Yet you rob me. "But you ask, 'How do we rob you?' "In tithes and offerings. 9 You are under a curse-the whole nation of you-because you are robbing me.

10 Bring the whole tithe into the storehouse, that there may be food in my house. Test me in this," says the LORD Almighty, "and see if I will not throw open the floodgates of heaven and pour out so much blessing that you will not have room enough for it. 11 I will prevent pests from devouring your crops, and the vines in your fields will not cast their fruit," says the LORD Almighty.

12 "Then all the nations will call you blessed, for yours will be a delight-ful land," says the LORD Almighty."

Kingdom Tithes and Offerings

God's Kingdom Economy

Establish your future right here and now in your present.

I will be using sowing and giving interchangeably in this book for simplicity. Before we move further into the major focus of this book, almsgiving, I wanted to share giving's broader umbrella that includes tithes and other offerings in addition to giving to the poor and needy in the family of God. God has defined a balance in our giving that helps sets the course for our life, the life of church leaders, your local and global church, the body of Christ and God's vast harvest field.

You have been given the power to set the course of your future by bringing your tithes and giving your offerings unto the household of God. God established tithes and offerings as a means to supply or bring to His people everything they need and abundantly more. God wants you to have what He has freely given you. When you give you are not giving to get just what you want, you are giving to get what God has for you; who is able to do immeasurably more than all we ask or imagine, according to his power that is at work within us. To Him is glory in the church and in Christ Jesus throughout all generations, for ever and ever! Amen. (Ephesians 3:20-21)

> Deuteronomy 12:6-7 "6 there bring ....., your tithes and special gifts, what you have vowed to give and your freewill offerings, and .... 7 There, in the presence of the LORD your God, you and your families shall eat and shall rejoice in everything you have put your hand to, because the LORD your God has blessed you. "

When we bring our tithes, 10% of the increase of our income, and give our offerings in the presence of the LORD we rejoice in everything because the LORD our God has blessed us! Tithes and offerings are a visual display of how God has blessed us. The tithe and offerings we present to the Lord is a reflection of the blessings God has bestowed upon us. We can only bring tithes to the Lord if we have been blessed with increase financially or materially. No increase, no tithe! However, when we do have increase we acknowledge the blessing given us by God and we joyously celebrate the gift of income from God by bringing our tithes unto Him. It is a time of reflection and thankfulness to God for providing for our need and abundantly more so. We remember His kindness toward us in supplying resources to us from the earth and giving us ability to increase. Therefore making a way for us to love God and love our neighbors by giving according to His word. Every week, on a Saturday, Sunday or the day of the week you gather with other believers to worship God, joyously bring your tithe celebrating God's gift of provision for you and your family. Take time to reflect on the 90% blessing income that God has given us to keep and use for our family's needs and the overflow to use for offerings, almsgivings to the poor and needy and short term and long term savings. Bless God from whom all blessings flow.

One problem many believers face is they concentrate on the tithe by looking at the 10% leaving their hands. They are looking at the tithe with dismay instead of looking at the blessing of the whole. The tithe is a part of the blessing of the whole. 100% or the whole of our income is given us by God and 10% or 1/10th part of the whole is the required tithe to bring back to God in obedience to His word. Stop looking at what leaves your hand and start looking at what comes into your hand, the whole of your income! Then you will be able to bring your tithes and give your offerings with a willing and rejoicing heart. How we look at or perceive Tithing can make all the difference in the world.

> Genesis 14:18-20   "18 Then Melchizedek king of Salem brought out bread and wine. He was priest of God Most High, 19 and he blessed Abram, saying, "Blessed be Abram by God Most High, Creator of heaven and earth. 20 And blessed be God Most High, who delivered your enemies into your hand." Then Abram gave him a tenth of everything. "

The first record of the tithe is found in Genesis 14:18-21, hundreds of years before the Law were given to Moses. The tithe was confirmed as a requirement for God's people as part of the Law (Leviticus 27:30).

The tithe continued to be expected to be bought to the priest during Jesus' earthly walk (Matthew 23:23) and it is still required today. God has never told us to stop tithing under the new covenant. Tithes are bought to the LORD to provide for His places of worship, His leaders and the people of God.

In Genesis 14:18-21, God began a pattern or foreshadow of things to come, showing us that the tithe is to be given to the priest establishing the link throughout the Bible between the tithe and the priest. In the Old Testament the covenant of Levi provided for the needs of the priests who were fulltime servants of the temple through tithes and offerings. (Deuteronomy 10: 8-9) This covenant guaranteed life and peace to the priest who honored God's word and taught the people to obey the truth. (Malachi 2:4-7)

As it was in the Beginning so it is also at the End

In the beginning, Melchizedek, the priest of the most high God, the King of Salem, received His tithe from Abraham. The King of Salem also means King of righteousness and King of peace. Jesus Christ, who is the righteous of God and the maker of peace, has been revealed to us as the high priest after the order of Melchizedek.

> Hebrews 6:19-20 "16 We have this hope as an anchor for the soul, firm and secure. It enters the inner sanctuary behind the curtain, 20where Jesus, who went before us, has entered on our behalf. He has become a high priest forever, in the order of Melchizedek."

God speaks of a priest who continually offers sacrifices and offerings before Him in Jeremiah 33:17-22, thus speaking of an eternal man who cannot die. Jesus Christ is the fulfillment of the eternal covenant that guarantees a man to stand before God continually in the office of priest.

> Jeremiah 33:17-22 "17 For this is what the LORD says: 'David will never fail to have a man to sit on the throne of the house of Israel, 18 nor will the priests, who are Levites, ever fail to have a man to stand before me continually to offer burnt

offerings, to burn grain offerings and to present sacrifices.' "19 The word of the LORD came to Jeremiah: 20 "This is what the LORD says: 'If you can break my covenant with the day and my covenant with the night, so that day and night no longer come at their appointed time, 21 then my covenant with David my servant—and my covenant with the Levites who are priests ministering before me—can be broken and David will no longer have a descendant to reign on his throne. 22 I will make the descendants of David my servant and the Levites who minister before me as countless as the stars of the sky and as measureless as the sand on the seashore.' "

There will always be a Priest before God continually

Jesus is the merciful and faithful high priest in service to God that He might make atonement for the sins of the people. (Hebrews 2:16-18b) Jesus Christ is the high priest, not under the Law of Moses because it was temporary, but He is the high priest under a changed law.

Hebrews 7:11-13   "11 If perfection could have been attained through the Levitical priesthood (for on the basis of it the law was given to the people), why was there still need for another priest to come-one in the order of Melchizedek, not in the order of Aaron? 12 For when there is a change of the priesthood, there must also be a change of the law. 13 He of whom these things are said belonged to a different tribe, and no one from that tribe has ever served at the altar."

In the one case, the tithe is collected by men who die (i.e. Leviticus Priesthood who are descendants of Abraham); but in the other case, the tithe is collected by him who is declared to be living. Jesus didn't become priest on the basis of a regulation or ancestry but on the basis of the power of an indestructible life:

Hebrews 7:15-21   "15 And what we have said is even more clear if another priest like Melchizedek appears, 16one who has become a priest not on the basis of a regulation as to his ancestry but on the basis of the power of an indestructible life. For it is declared: "You are a priest forever, in the order of

Melchizedek." 18 The former regulation is set aside because it was weak and useless 19(for the law made nothing perfect), and a better hope is introduced, by which we draw near to God. 20 And it was not without an oath! Others became priests without any oath, 21 but he became a priest with an oath when God said to him:

"The Lord has sworn and will not change his mind: 'You are a priest forever.'"

By oath the Lord has sworn, Jesus has become the guarantee of a better covenant. (Psalm 110:4) Under the Law death prevented priest from continuing in office but because Jesus lives forever, He has a permanent priesthood. Therefore He is able to save completely those who come to God through Him, because He always lives to intercede for them. (Hebrews 7:22-25). There is no doubt the lesser is blessed by the greater. (Hebrews 7:7) Under the better covenant we who are the lesser bring tithes in the presence of the greater, our great high priest Jesus Christ. We are to bless the greater still today. Out of gratefulness for the blessings Jesus Christ has bestowed upon us, we bring our tithes and give our offerings under the New Covenant also.

Offerings, the Complement of the Tithe

God said to bring our tithes and offerings to the storehouse of God. (Malachi 3:10) Bringing our tithes to the Lord is not the end of the story as some think; God also requires offerings from all He has given to us. We freely give our offerings because God has freely given to us. Think about that! Out of thankfulness to God, we give back to him a portion of what He has given to us.

There are special times appointed by the LORD to give offerings. God has defined both "required" offerings and volunteer offerings. "Required" offerings don't have a set amount but they do have a set time on God's calendar and a set place to be given. Volunteer offerings are given out of our freewill such as Alms offerings to the poor and needy, vows or pledges to contribute to a worthy cause, and freewill offerings given during worship gatherings. Volunteer offerings do not have a set time on God's calendar or a set amount as defined by the Bible.

God's appointed times of offerings:

God set aside special feast days or weeks in the Spring and Fall on the Hebrew calendar to give offerings required by Him. When we learn God's Holy calendar and follow His ways, which are greater than our ways, we will be blessed as God has commanded when we bring our offerings at the appointed times.

> Leviticus 23:3-4, 14   "3 Speak unto the children of Israel, and say unto them, concerning the feasts of the LORD, which ye shall proclaim to be holy convocations, even these are MY FEASTS... 4. These are the FEASTS OF THE LORD, even holy convocations, which ye shall proclaim in their seasons.".................. This is to be a lasting ordinance for the generations to come, wherever you live."

These appointed, memorial feasts or holy convocations of our Almighty God are celebrated in both the Old and New Testaments.

> Matt 26:17-19 "17 On the first day of the Feast of Unleavened Bread, the disciples came to Jesus and asked, "Where do you want us to make preparations for you to eat the Passover?" 18 He replied, "Go into the city to a certain man and tell him, 'The Teacher says: My appointed time is near. I am going to celebrate the Passover with my disciples at your house.'" 19 So the disciples did as Jesus had directed them and prepared the Passover. "

The Spring Feast

- The Feast of Passover - (Exodus 12:1-14, Matthew 26:18-19, 1 Corinthians 5:7)

- The Feast of Unleavened Bread — (Leviticus 23:5-8, Deuteronomy 16:3, Luke 22:19, 2 Chronicles 30:21-27)

- The Feast of First Fruits (Deut. 26:1-11, 1 Corinthians 15:20-23, James 1:18)

- The Feast of weeks or Pentecost (meaning 50 days) – (Leviticus 23:15-17, Acts 2:1-4)

Deut 16:16-17 "16 Three times a year all your men must appear before the LORD your God at the place he will choose: at the Feast of Unleavened Bread, the Feast of Weeks and the Feast of Tabernacles. No man should appear before the LORD empty-handed: 17 Each of you must bring a gift in proportion to the way the LORD your God has blessed you."

The Fall Feast

- The Feast of Trumpets — (Leviticus. 23:23-25, Matthew 24:31, Revelations 11:15)

- The Feast of Atonement — (Leviticus 23:26-32, Romans 3:25, Hebrews 2:17).

- The Feast of Tabernacles — (Leviticus 23:33-43, Revelations 21:3)

Many Christians might be saying why are you speaking of feast days and offerings required in the Old Testament? Aren't these holy days and offerings required only of those under the Law? Since we aren't under the Old Covenant commandments shouldn't you be talking about God's required holy days and offerings under the New Covenant? God's holy feast days are not just for those under the Old Covenant. They have rich symbolism designed to point us to God's protection, redemption, provision, salvation, wisdom and worship in Jesus Christ. They also give us a wonderful visual to help us remember and teach God's mighty work on earth both under the Old Covenants and the New. These feast days and offerings are a time of celebration, honor, praise and worship to our almighty and wise God. God calls His covenant people together for appointed times throughout the year. Participating in these feast days will not earn anyone a place in heaven. Additionally, no one will go to hell simply because they choose not to participate in God's appointed feast days. We are to let no man place on us requirements for our salvation that Christ has not given us. (Colossians 2:13-17)   For those who have already received God's salvation, these feast days and special offerings are for God's people to remember and praise and honor Him for:

> ⇒   His mighty hand of redemption and salvation (Feast of Passover, Unleavened Bread)

> ⇒   Jesus' blood sacrifice forgiving our sin (Feast of Unleavened Bread, Atonement)

> ⇒   Jesus Christ who dwells (tabernacles) with us and in us (Feast of Tabernacles)

> ⇒   Eternal Life and Christ Return for His Church (Feast of Trumpets)

> ⇒   His Spiritual Blessings of Life and Prosperity (Feast of First Fruits and Pentecost)

We should all take the time to remember what God has done for us. What better time than at God's appointed times. Our Father is looking for those who would worship Him in Spirit and in Truth everyday and this includes worshipping Him together during His special holy days.

I can understand the line of thought that says since we are under the New Covenant we don't have to honor the feast days and offerings given to Israel. I used to think the same way until the night of February 21, 2007. For 3 hours long from 10:00 pm to 1:00 am God taught me about His principles of Sabbath Rest, His Spring Feast and His offerings between Passover and Pentecost. To summarize the 3 hours, God spoke to me about the 777 Blessing; For 7 Sabbaths of weeks, I was commanded to give 7 offerings of $7.00 (or $49) to each of 7 ministries of God's choice. The amazing thing about this teaching is God taught me about obedience to His appointed times when I was relatively ignorant to God's eternal feast. God taught me about His feast exactly 7 Sabbaths or 49 days before the start of the 1st of the Spring feast, Passover.   The 7th Sabbath fell on April 7, 2007, the day before the 50th day of the celebration of Passover 2007. God prepared me to celebrate His spring feast with wisdom and faith foreshadowing to me His feast requirements before the official start of Passover 2007. I was prepared with revelation to celebrate God's festivals at His appointed times. Praise God!

Obedience to the 777 Blessing revelation bought astounding blessings to my family's life. My husband, Frank, is the head coach of a Public High School football team in Delaware. This High School has never won a state championship nor had they ever been in a championship game before. They went undefeated for the first time in school history, becoming the first team in the state to go 13-0 and they won the championship. My husband won coach of the year and became the first African American to win a football title in our state. My husband's heart in coaching was changed that year to give the glory in winning or loosing to God. He passed his beliefs to the assistant coaches, to the players and all other members of the team. Supernaturally the team followed my husband's godly coaching philosophy and the result was evident in the spirit of the team, the perfect season and the many records and rewards the team and coach received. To God is the Glory.

Changing the way we think to the way God thinks brings supernatural favor, mercy and grace toward us. We can do what man thinks is impossible in Christ Jesus. God has tremendously favored our family and our church family with wisdom, revelation, open doors, family love, and an increase of love, honor and respect for God. God has been here for us, He has healed us and He has provided for us. God wants to be with you and bless you. He wants to dwell with and tabernacle with you. Won't you let Him? Turn to Him and Follow Him. Let God's thoughts and ways guide you into all truth. God is the one who has something to say about that. Listen to Him and live in the blessing.

Celebrating God's eternal feasts brings joy and prosperity to His people.

Deuteronomy 16:15 "For seven days celebrate the Feast to the LORD your God at the place the LORD will choose. For the LORD your God will bless you in all your harvest and in all the work of your hands, and your joy will be complete."

Lev 23:41 "Celebrate this as a festival to the LORD for seven days each year. This is to be a lasting ordinance for the generations to come; celebrate it in the seventh month."

Our Lord, Jesus Christ celebrated the feast days.

John 2:13, 23 "13 When it was almost time for the Jewish Passover, Jesus went up to Jerusalem. 23 Now while he was in Jerusalem at the Passover Feast, many people saw the miraculous signs he was doing and believed in his name."

The apostle Paul celebrated the feast days.

Acts 20:16 "Paul had decided to sail past Ephesus to avoid spending time in the province of Asia, for he was in a hurry to reach Jerusalem, if possible, by the day of Pentecost."

Giving tithes and appointed times offerings is just the beginning with God. We have not arrived at our destination in the Lord because we consistently give our tithes and offerings. There are no bragging rights here. Hold on to your seat though, because as one who tithes you have received Kingdom blessings as a result of your obedience to God. Following God helps us to operate in His divine promises and achieve God's purposes for our life. We are not to rob God of His tithes and offerings. God wants us to be well rounded believers; to tithe, give offerings, and to impart justice, and mercy and show His love to the World. God had something to say about that in Matthew 23:23 when He rebuked the Pharisees, teachers of the law, for touting their pride in tithing every increase even the smallest of all garden herbs but they neglected to display the love of God.

> Matt 23:23 "Woe to you, teachers of the law and Pharisees, you hypocrites! You give a tenth of your spices-mint, dill and cumin. But you have neglected the more important matters of the law-justice, mercy and faithfulness. You should have practiced the latter, without neglecting the former."

God doesn't expect anything of His children that He doesn't first display Himself. God is a giver and has given the greatest gift of all in His Son Jesus Christ. God designed us to be made in the image of

Him; we too are designed by our Maker to be givers. God is Love. He displays His love to us in forgiving our sins even though we were enemies of His and He expects us to show this same manner of His love to the world. God expects us to display His love that was poured into us by the power of the Holy Spirit (Rom 5:5) by showing mercy to the undeserved, by showing justice to the oppressed and mistreated, wrongfully imprisoned, and to righteously carry out the full council of His Word on earth. Love is the foundation of giving, outreach, and forgiveness. God is love and without love our work does not prosper. Without putting God's love into practice our heart reflects only what's most important to us and not what's most important to God. Remember, only what we do for God will last.

Love moves us to give voluntarily.

Psalm 61:8 "Then will I ever sing praise to your name and fulfill my vows day after day."

Alms and Freewill giving and making a vow to give are all in the category of volunteer offerings. But don't relax too quickly because God commands us to give to the poor through alms offerings.

Deuteronomy 15:11 "There will always be poor people in the land. Therefore I command you to be openhanded toward your brothers and toward the poor and needy in your land."

God doesn't tell us when to give or how much to give, thus making this offering voluntary but He does expect us to give.

Alms are gifts to the poor, needy and weak who are in lack and need to be supplied.

Freewill offerings are simply given out of your free will. Many times it's a spontaneous gift given at the request of someone or some organization. When there is a request to contribute to a weekly church worship gathering, new church building, a fundraiser event, a scholarship fund or the like, they are requesting a freewill offering. The recipient of the gift is expecting us to give an offering based solely on what we freely decide with our heart and mind, willingly and abundantly.

A **Vow or pledge** to give is a spoken or written communication of commitment to give financially or materially to someone or to a group sometime in the future. It's a promise to give a certain amount before you actually give it. A vow should not be made lightly but with much thought ensuring you are able to give what you promised out of your mouth before you commit to a vow.

> Deuteronomy 23:23 "Whatever your lips utter you must be sure to do, because you made your vow freely to the LORD your God with your own mouth."

God doesn't tell us when to make a vow or how much to vow, we determine this ourselves; it's voluntary. But when we do make a vow, God requires us to keep our vows and when we do not, it is a sin.

> Deuteronomy 23:21 "If you make a vow to the LORD your God, do not be slow to pay it, for the LORD your God will certainly demand it of you and you will be guilty of sin."

In this book we will be focusing on Volunteer offerings i.e. a pledged vow to give alms offerings to the worthy cause of giving to the poor and needy saints in Jerusalem based on 2 Corinthians 9. All offerings defined in the Bible are important. We will not be speaking directly of tithing or special appointed feast times offerings in this book, but no other giving can replace the tithe or the feast offerings of the Bible. God's way is for believers to bring our tithes and give our feast offerings in addition to giving our Alms offerings. Our giving is to be presented to God in the following way:

1st: The tithe = 10% of all our increase

2nd: Special God Appointed Feast offerings as set by God in His Word

3rd: Volunteer offerings

- such as vows to contribute to a worthy cause

- Alms offerings given to help the needy, poor, oppressed, imprisoned, etc.

- Freewill offerings such as what we give during a worship service or to ministries above the tithe

Hebrews 13:16 "And do not forget to do good and to share with others, for with such sacrifices God is pleased."

Tithe and Offering Questions and Answers

Q. Isn't the tithe in the Law of Moses? I thought since Jesus Christ came we are no longer required to pay the tithe.

A. Satan has really thrown in a boat load of confusion into the body of Christ when it comes to tithes and offerings. Many believe tithes are of the Old Testament only and not the New Testament. Jesus speaks of continuing to tithe in the New Testament in Matthew 23:23. The tithe was upheld by Jesus and is right to bring today.

Q. What is a tithe? The church I attend says if I consistently give any amount I am tithing is this true?

A. The tithe means a tenth part or 10% of all our increase of income.

Q. Do we bring tithes out of gross or net pay?

A. Tithe 10% of your gross income. We are to tithe off all our increase of income not part of it. Reducing our increase of income by what we pay the government in taxes reduces our overall tithe of our income causing us to rob God of His tithe. Give unto Caesar what is Caesar's and to God what is God's.

(Matthew 22:21) The government doesn't come first, God does.

Q. What is considered an increase of income? How do I know what income to tithe and not to tithe?

A. Anytime we get additional income we have not previously tithed on, reserve God's 10% out of it every time. Some examples are income received from:

- full time or part time jobs,

- monetary gifts received,

- money made from a hobby or a side job,

- money made under the table or over the table,

- profit made from investments

- profit from the sale of something.

Please note this is not an exhaustive list.

Q. Who should be the recipient of alms?

A. Give as God instructs you! He may have a special mission for you. Remember also what the Bible says: give to those who are in need, lacking or poor.

- Especially to our Covenanted Family of God in Jesus Christ (this includes the Jews)

- We must not neglect our blood family

- And after you have supplied the need of the two above then others as you purpose in your heart

Q. How much offering do I give? Is there a standard percentage to give?

A. This is really up to you. If you have plenty share it. When you give to the needy be generous.

Q. What is the God's primary purpose for bringing tithes and giving offerings?

A. The primary purpose is to provide for the needs of God's people such as the basic needs of food, clothing and shelter to God's anointed leaders, teachers and missionaries who have no other means of support. Specifically God wants fulltime ministers to give their time to His word and thus support from tithes and offerings provide them the time to do so. In Israel God accomplish this by everyone bringing tithes every year and every three years of their agricultural harvest to the grain storehouse of God to feed the Levites (The teachers of the Law), widows, the fatherless, the poor and the alien (Deuteronomy 14:28, 29) God also shows this purpose through the sharing of the blessings of a portion of the fall and spring harvest with all of Israel at His appointed feast time celebrations. In this way God has established 3 times a year when everyone in Israel could provide for one another's needs. (Exodus 23:14-16)

Q. What if I have not paid a vow in the past, now that I know the truth can I pay it now?

A. Yes and ask God to forgive your past sin and He will forgive you.

Q. Can a vow be canceled?

A. The word of God says to never make vows rashly without significant thought. Once you make a vow it is expected of you to pay it with 2 exceptions: (see Exodus 20:1-11)

1.   If you are a daughter living in your father's house and your father doesn't agree with the vow you have committed to, he can cancel your vow and you no longer are obligated to pay it.

2.   If you are a married women and your husband doesn't agree with the vow you have committed to, he can cancel the vow.

Men and all other women are obligated to fulfill all vows made out of their mouths.

Q. I made a vow in the emotion of a church convention; it was a mistake to make this vow. Am I obligated to pay it?

A. Yes you are even though it was made rashly and without thought. It is better to not vow than to make a vow and not fulfill it.

Ecclesiastes 5:6 "Do not let your mouth lead you into sin. And do protest to the temple messenger, "My vow was a mistake." Why should God be angry at what you say and destroy the work of your hands?"

Do your best to fulfill your vow. But if your mouth has led you into sin, ask God to forgive you of your sin and Jesus Christ our intercessor will forgive you of all your unrighteousness and cleanse and purify you from your sin. When you are forgiven, do not sin again with your mouth in making a rash vow. We must be in awe of God and not promise Him something we cannot fulfill.

Q. I have tried in the past to consistently tithe but sooner or later something happens and I either reduce my giving or stop for a while. How can I overcome this problem and give regularly as my heart desires?

A. Let God forgive you and forgive yourself if you failed in the past to consistently give or do fail in the future. Submit yourself to God, repent and allow Jesus to cleanse you from all unrighteousness. Brush yourself off, get up and start again with renewed determination to follow God faithfully in all you're giving.

Here are a few tidbits that could help you:

•   Separate your giving out of your income immediately upon receiving it. Do not spend any of your income until you separate the giving from your spending and your savings. One suggestion is to open a separate account for your giving, a separate account for your savings and a separate spending account. If possible have your tithe, offerings, and alms directly deposited into your bank account so it doesn't have to go through your hands. Don't get an ATM card for your giving account. Only get the minimum amount of checks for this account and only use the checks when you are bringing your tithes, paying your vows and/or giving your offerings or alms.

•   When you receive your paycheck obligate yourself to 90% of your paycheck only. If you make $1000.00, don't make plans for $1000.00, instead make plans for $900.00 or less and this way you won't find yourself eating into your tithe and offerings destroying your future harvest.

Have the attitude, the tenth or the tithe is not mine, it's God's and I will not rob Him by mistake or even deliberately.   So plan ahead of time to reserve for God what's His.

•   Read your Bible daily searching diligently for scriptures about giving. He who thirsts after righteousness will be filled. (Matthew 5:6) Pray often for the fruit of the Spirit of self discipline and then practice disciplining yourself in giving.

•   With God's help determine what you will give and give it. Your mind will try to reason away the decision that's in your heart but don't give in. There's a righteous harvest waiting for you. Listen to the Holy Spirit in you. Listening to God brings about a righteous harvest far exceeding the satisfaction we may receive from giving our own way or keeping our money in our pockets. This really comes down to whom do you trust more, God or yourself?

Proverbs 3:5-10 sums it up masterfully:

> "5 Trust in the LORD with all your heart
>
> and lean not on your own understanding;
>
> 6 in all your ways acknowledge him,
>
> and he will make your paths straight.
>
> 7 Do not be wise in your own eyes;
>
> fear the LORD and shun evil.
>
> 8 This will bring health to your body
>
> and nourishment to your bones.
>
> 9 Honor the LORD with your wealth,
>
> with the firstfruits of all your crops;
>
> 10 then your barns will be filled to overflowing,
>
> and your vats will brim over with new wine"

3rd John 2

"Beloved, I wish above all things that thou mayest prosper

and be in health, even as thy soul prospereth." KJV

Kingdom Revelation and Instructions

One Sunday morning I was preparing breakfast in the midst of a snow storm. Our church worship service was canceled and I was worshiping our Lord with singing and praising. Joy filled my soul and a familiar sense of peace and calm was in the air. It was the Holy Spirit. God spoke and I listened. God's revealed word to me was clear and certain. He said:

"I want you to tell my people the truth about 2 Corinthians chapter 9. My people reason too much."

Believers, we are to live by the truth; by every word that proceeds out of the mouth of God. God wants His children to be obedient to the words He spoke through Paul in 2 Corinthians 9. His people have reasoned too much for too long about this text of scripture and God wants it to cease. Too much reasoning has caused God's people to miss the prosperity that accompanies submitting to the truth. God wants His blessings to flow toward you. Listen to the word of the Lord, obey it and be blessed.

God sealed His word to me with this scripture:

3 John 2 "Beloved, I wish above all things that thou mayest prosper and be in health, even as thy soul prospereth." KJV

Our soul prospers when our mind is transformed by the truth of God. We prosper and are in good health when our mind is free from the conformity of this world and the power of reasoning too much that sways us away from faithfully obeying God. Receiving God's revelation, possessing it as our own and acting on the instructions bring the power of God on the earth and prosperity toward us. Revelation combined with instructions from God shakes believers at our very core prompting us to action that turns the world up side down. Change is inevitable. Revelation and instructions (i.e. the when, where, and how to carry out the revelation) acted upon will change a situation, move a mountain, over come a barrier and heal a matter. God sends His revelation (i.e. His revealed word of knowledge and wisdom) to His people to unify us in His one will, one cause and one purpose in the earth; this is how we know what God wants to happen in the earth.

Matthew 6:9-10 "9 Our Father, which art in heaven, Hallowed be thy name, 10 Thy kingdom come, thy will be done in earth as it is in heaven."

Revelation from God brings blessings to the people of the earth and glory to our Father in heaven. God's blessings of healing and prosperity, was bestowed upon a barren woman's womb because revelation and instruction was given to me for the perfect will of heaven to manifest on earth. This story is amazing. She and her husband had attempted many times to bring a child into this world but were unsuccessful. She had multiple miscarriages and because of this they were warned sternly by their doctor to not try again to get pregnant because it would be dangerous to her health and possibly her life. They were getting older and passed the age of adoption in their state. They were a couple with no hope until God intervened. God flew me across the country from Delaware to Colorado when I was 4 months pregnant to speak a word of revelation that would turn their world upside down and heal the matter that burdened and discouraged them. My pregnant belly wasn't showing quite yet but she sensed I was pregnant and she began sharing her and her husband's burden and sadness with me. I could empathize with their burdened because five months earlier I too experienced a miscarriage. And we know God works for the good of those who love him and have been called according to his purpose. (Rom 8:28) After she poured out her heart, I shared with her the one I knew who could heal her body. She was excited and opened to hear who this person was! I revealed to her, Jesus Christ, the healer was the person she and her husband needed. She remained curious and we talked about Jesus that night. God gave me John 20:21-23 to pray for her and I followed His instructions even though I knew nothing about their personal life. I prayed for both her and her husband's sins to be forgiven according to John 20:21-23 and the healing of her womb. I left her a note of encouragement the next day and I traveled back to Delaware. Approximately 10 months after our conversation in Colorado she gave birth to a beautiful healthy baby boy.

This true story is an example of how when God's revelation and instructions are obeyed, the windows of heaven open up and blessings flow in the earth. Just as I heeded to the revelation and instructions that provided much needed healing to the womb of this barren woman, I also have heeded to the revealed word and instructions of God to write this book. We should expect nothing less than the outpouring of God's prosperity and healing for all of us who will allow God to prosper our souls with his truth about 2 Corinthians 9.

Our God given Capacity to Reason must be in Service to God's Revelation

Revelation 3:6 "He who has an ear, let him hear what the Spirit says to the churches"

God has something to say to the churches. God wants the hearer to listen and to follow the revealed word that is coming forth out of His mouth. Some in the church will "turn on" their listening ears and hear the word of our Lord and submit their capacity to reason to the service of God. They allow God to transform their minds leading them to be over comers. Good! We overcome by faith in Jesus Christ, the revealed Word of God. He who has an ear to hear operates in faith that seeks to understand God's perfect will and follow it.

Still others in the church will hear the revealed word but will choose to "turn off" their listening ears and choose not to submit their reasoning capacity to the service of God. They reject His truth and trust in their thoughts and ways. These are those who are unfaithful because they exalt their words above God's Word. A lot of times this is because they have a "prove it to me" attitude before they will launch out in faith. They won't believe it until they see it. These believers trust in their own understanding more than they trust in God's.

We are to trust in God!

Proverbs 3:5-6 "5 Trust in the LORD with all your heart and lean not on your own understanding; 6 in all your ways acknowledge him, and he will make your paths straight."

Without realizing it, believers who lean on their own understanding have just made their thoughts and reason an idol when they put them above God. 2 Corinthians 10:3-6 speaks directly to this very problem; stating every imagination, stronghold, and high thing that exalts itself above the knowledge of God will be cast down and every thought will be bought into captivity to the obedience of Christ. The high minded will be bought low and the lowly or humble will be exalted. Don't worry, God has patience and we have hope that faith comes by hearing and hearing by the Word of God. Thus causing us to agree with God and serve Him only, just as we professed when we received Jesus Christ as Lord and Savior.

God has revealed, we are commanded to give to the poor and needy. Do we have the faith to put our reason where it belongs to carry out God's command? Will we submit our reason to the service of God in giving? Or will we allow our money, power, status or the desire for them to cloud our judgment when revelation to give is sent from heaven. When God says to give, sometimes our thoughts turn to keeping what we have. Most people have a will to give, to love, to share and to help. This is true for those who have and those who have not. As we move on in our life it seems our desires to give and to do for others, many times get overshadowed by our strong and compelling want to acquire things that helps us reach our lifestyle goals. However, we soon find that in our acquiring of many things, it takes time, money and energy to maintain our current lifestyle and much effort to continuously improve it. A conflict of desires arises between the desire to give and the desire to maintain or improve our status quo of living. God wants us to channel our reasoning capacity to understanding and submitting to His word instead of focusing on preserving our status quo.

We have the power to submit our reason to God. We can do this because God has given us the ability to conceive and reason the word of God. God has written His word on our hearts and in our minds. (Hebrews 8:10) Thus enabling us to reject conformity of our minds to the patterns of this world and move us toward agreeing with God. Wherefore our minds are transformed to operate in the perfect will of God in our giving.

Romans 12:1-3 " 1 Therefore, I urge you, brothers, in view of God's mercy, to offer your bodies as living sacrifices, holy and pleasing to God—this is your spiritual act of worship. 2Do not conform any longer to the pattern of this world, but be transformed by the renewing of your mind. Then you will be able to test and approve what God's will is—his good, pleasing and perfect will."

God created our minds to think and He expects us to use our transformed minds. He didn't create us as robots but gave us thought and choice. I don't want anyone to conclude that revelation and thinking don't mix. There are some church cultures that believe higher level Christian education, such as Bible Schools or Seminaries somehow quench the direction of the Holy Spirit in the believer's life. Attendees of these schools are often called thinkers or intellectuals, and it's not said in a favorable light. But God is not an anti-intellectual or against thinking. What would that say then about God, who has given us anointed teachers to mature the saints of God for works of service? (Ephesians 4:12). Teachers help our minds and hearts transform to God's way of thinking. God raises up Godly teachers in many places, in church buildings, in our neighborhoods, in schools, etc. God is the creator of human thought. God gives us reason and intends for us to use it whether we are in school or not. Reasoning is to be in partnership with God not opposed to Him.

Isaiah 1:18 "Come now, let us reason together," says the LORD.

When we received Jesus Christ we became a new creation in Him and this new creation requires a new way of thinking; all things become new even the requirements of our mind. We are to let God show us the way to prosperous thinking. God desires to move us from our level of reasoning to operating in His realm of revelation. We can only achieve God's desire when we submit our God given ability to reason or think under His revelation.

2 Corinthians 9 is all about Kingdom Business

The Kingdom principles found in 2 Corinthians 9 directly speak to the God given grace that causes prosperity for God's people, and the humble and righteous submission to the gospel of Jesus Christ that produces praise, honor, glory and thanksgiving to God.

The Kingdom of God is Open for Business

Will you enter through the open door and partake of God's divine promises and reap of His holy fruit? Or will you stand outside the doorway window shopping. Looking but not buying, wishing but not taking action, dreaming but not realizing one foot forward will get you through the door into God's world. It is greater than anything you could ever imagine or ask for.

Luke 17:20-21 "The kingdom of God does not come with your careful observation, 21 nor will people say, 'Here it is,' or 'There it is,' because the kingdom of God is within you."

Everything we need can be found in the Kingdom of God. The Kingdom of God is inside us. But we tend to look outside the Kingdom inside us for the answer to our needs.

John 18:36 Jesus said, "My kingdom is not of this world. If it were, my servants would fight to prevent my arrest by the Jews. But now my kingdom is from another place."

Children of God, It's All in the Kingdom

Citizens of Heaven, children of God our help comes from the LORD and through the people of His Kingdom. Let us take our rightful place in the Kingdom of God. Let us stop looking for the world to provide for us and even rescue us and start looking to the King of the Kingdom, Jesus Christ, for our every provision. God wants us to know He is quite able to fully support and provide for His children out of His Kingdom! "Do not be afraid, little flock, for your Father has been pleased to give you the kingdom. Luke 12:32

The Kingdom of His Son:

Colossians 1:12-14, 16-18 "12 giving thanks to the Father, who has qualified you to share in the inheritance of the saints in the kingdom of light. 13 For he has rescued us from the dominion of darkness and brought us into the kingdom of the Son he loves... 16 For by him all things were created: things in heaven and on earth, visible and invisible, whether thrones or powers or rulers or authorities; all things were created by him and for him. 17 He is before all things, and in him all things hold together. 18 And he is the head of the body, the church; he is the beginning and the firstborn from among the dead, so that in everything he might have the supremacy."

In all things Christ, the King of the Kingdom has preeminence. He is in charge. He is the head of all things, creator of all things and by Him all things have their being. He is the head of the church and all things have been placed under his feet; the fullness of Christ fills everything in everyway for the believer. This Kingdom we are speaking of is within us. This means the fullness of Christ is within us. The one who creates all things is able to create for us all the things that we need. All of our needs will be met according to the glorious riches of God's grace in Christ Jesus. Provision is found within us and not outside of us in this world. When we pray to God we must know that the Kingdom of God is where we are expecting our provision.

Believers, we have all things in Common in the Kingdom of God. (Acts 2:44) God wants us to take our rightful place in the Kingdom of God by Excelling in the Grace of Giving according to the revelation and instruction given us in 2 Corinthians chapter 9.

2 Corinthians 8:7 "But just as you excel in everything-in faith, in speech, in knowledge, in complete earnestness and in your love for us- see that you also excel in this grace of giving."

Believers let us resolve to take our rightful place in the Kingdom of God. Let us reflect on a poem God gave me to help guide us:

I'm Taking My Rightful Place in the Kingdom of God

I am God's child and
I am taking my rightful place in the Kingdom of God.

I want to be satisfied in the morning by God's unfailing Love,
I want my heart to be penetrated by God's wisdom and knowledge
from above.
I will not be blocked by anyone, anything or in any way;
I receive and I am not deceived. It is my right to walk in His light.

I am God's child and
I'm taking my rightful place in the Kingdom of God.

I receive every Spiritual blessing in the Heavenly realms;
Yes all things are placed under Christ Jesus feet,
For it is impossible for me to walk in defeat.
In Christ it is my right to be lifted up by His might.

I am God's child and
I'm taking my rightful place in the Kingdom of God.

I receive God's good purpose to will and act in my life;
I want God to establish the work of my hands,
His favor rest upon me continuously as only He can.
The Word of God gives me the right to walk by faith and not by
sight.

I am God's child and
I'm taking my rightful place in the Kingdom of God.

It is for God's good pleasure that I am created;
It is the power of God working in me, through me and out of me,
establishing my life eternally.
Sealed with the Holy Spirit, I'm guaranteed this right,
The victory is mine; Jesus won the fight.

I am God's Child and
I'm taking my rightful place in the Kingdom of God.

2 Corinthians 9:12-15

"12 This service that you perform is not only supplying the needs of

God's people but is also overflowing in many expressions of thanks to

God. 13 Because of the service by which you have proved yourselves,

men will praise God for the obedience that accompanies your

confession of the gospel of Christ, and for your generosity in sharing

with them and with everyone else. 14 And in their prayers for you their

hearts will go out to you, because of the surpassing grace God has

given you.

15 Thanks be to God for his indescribable gift!"

Who will be kind to the poor? (Proverbs 28:8b)

There are two chapters in 2 Corinthians, chapters 8 and 9, devoted to encourage Gentile believers in the Church at Achaia, which is on the Gulf of Corinth, to freely and willingly contribute financially and materially to a collection that would provide for the needs of the poor saints in Jerusalem.

God has something to say about that...

These 2 chapters and many others in the Bible teach God's people how to manage money and possessions by showing us their true use and purposes in the earth.

How we use our given resources will determine our treasures on earth and in heaven. God wants to reward everyone who has faith in Him and His Word. There is one problem; God has revealed "we reason too much" in this area. Our spirit is willing but our flesh is weak. Our mind "reasons too much" and causes us to submit to the flesh instead of submitting to the will of the Spirit in our use of money and possessions.

One of the hardest areas to be transformed in a believer's life is our attitude or perspective about money and its intended use. Our attitude about money and its use can prevent the will of heaven from being done in our lives on earth. The Parable of the rich young ruler, in Luke 18:18-29, whom excelled at being obedient to every commandment, ordinance and statue of the law of God given to Moses from birth, requested of the Good Master Jesus, what must he do to gain eternal life? The Good Master Jesus' answered, "...You still lack one thing. Sell your possessions and give them to the poor, and you will have treasure in heaven. Then come and follow me". (Luke 18:22) The Father's will in heaven was for this young ruler to come into the eternal Kingdom. This rich young ruler who excelled at everything else was not able to master the one thing he needed to do to obtain eternal life. He couldn't bring himself to change his perspective about money and possessions. The new revelation given to this rich young ruler, to come follow Jesus, was conditional upon him changing his view about his earthly wealth. Jesus' concern for us is not foremost earthly wealth but heavenly wealth. In Christ we have every Spiritual Blessing in the heavenly realms. Yet we are stuck in desiring and some even excelling in obtaining every material blessing in the earthly realm. Our minds need to be transformed into Kingdom thinking in order to excel at gaining treasure in heaven.

The church at Achaia in Corinth had a similar resume to the rich young ruler. They were commended for excelling in faith, in utterance (expressing themselves), in knowledge and in all diligence (zeal), and in their love for the disciples and Apostles of God. They were also financially well off. There was still one area they were being tested in and the verdict for how they would respond to this test was still out. Would they do as the rich young ruler did, excel in most things but fail in mastering money? The danger here is this, if we don't learn to master money, money will master us. Would the Corinthian's try to serve two masters, just as the rich young ruler did, trying to serve both God and money? God said we can't serve two masters, we will love one and hate the other or else we will despise the one and hold on to the other. (Matthew 6:24) The rich young ruler chose to hold money as his master and to despise the other, whom he himself called "the Good Master Jesus". The rich young ruler lacked one thing and that was submitting his finances to God. This one thing, kept him from entering the eternal Kingdom of God. Believers who choose not to submit their finances to God will not enter into the full blessings of the Kingdom of God. There is not one believer who is willing to leave his finances and material possessions in the hands of God for the Kingdom of God's sake who will not receive much more on this earth and in eternal life.

Luke 18:29-30 29 "I tell you the truth," Jesus said to them, "no one who has left home or wife or brothers or parents or children for the sake of the kingdom of God 30 will fail to receive many times as much in this age and, in the age to come, eternal life."

Did the Church at Achaia believe the sayings of Jesus? Did they really believe giving of their finances to help the poor saints in Jerusalem for the sake of the Kingdom of God, that they would receive back much more than they gave? Did they understand they would not just be limited to earthly gain but much more also in the world to come life everlasting?

Their actions and not just their words would prove their true beliefs.

The Test!

Would the church at Corinth's actions align with God's will or their will? This is the test of every believer! We are faced daily with whether to choose God's way or our way. Every believer will be tested to determine if they choose God's way of handling money or their own way. God's way for the church at Corinth at this time was to contribute to the fund being collected for the poor in Jerusalem. They had already vowed a year ago to contribute. Are they still willing to contribute? What would they contribute? Would they submit to God to determine the amount God wants them to give? This is a challenge and a test to us all. Would they pass the test?

The Apostle Paul and other disciples didn't want to take the chance that the church at Corinth wouldn't pass the test. Therefore, Paul wrote this letter of encouragement (2 Corinthians 9) and sent disciples to witness to them with the goal of preparing for the offering before the actual collection date. The witnesses shared testimonies of churches that followed through on their vows, even those who were poor. Would the testimony of the Church at Macedonia spur them on to reflect the same grace of God in their gift? Would they allow the grace of God to push them beyond their current comfort zone in giving? Would they be able to rise above the realm of their lack into a new realm of excelling in almsgiving and fulfilling their previous vow? God is no respecter of persons. The grace He gave to the Church of Macedonia is also available to the church at Achaia and to us. God's grace taught the Church of Macedonia to turn from their thoughts and ways of giv-ing and turn to God's righteous way. When they submitted to God's grace, their contribution to the fund even astounded the Apostles and disciples who were leading the collection. How could these believer's who were poor themselves contribute so much? The only explanation was that the very power of the grace of God enabled Macedonia to do beyond what anyone was expecting. The grace of God enabled them to see beyond their affliction and poverty and respond with an abundance of joy to give a gift to help the poor saints in Jerusalem. The churches at Macedonia were very willing to trust God to sow the seed needed to help the poor. They followed a pattern we too need to follow when asked to give to help our brethren in Christ. (2 Corinthians 8:1-5)

1.   They were first willing to give.

2.   They gave their hearts to God for Him to determine their ability to give.

3.   They didn't let their current circumstances dictate their contribution.

4.   They allowed God's grace to work in them abundantly, enabling them to supply the needs of their brethren in Jerusalem even beyond the expectations of man.

Submitting our finances to God will enable us to see beyond our self, our family, and our desires and enable us to see the needs of others as well as our own needs. Even more it will position us to reflect the work of Jesus in our life. Jesus, although He was rich, yet for our sakes He became poor, that we through His poverty might be rich. (2 Corinthians 8:9 paraphrased)

Now from the truth as we glean from the letter in 2 Corinthians chapters 8 and 9, the church at Achaia was very willing to contribute to the fund for the poor saints in Jerusalem. They already passed the first test. They had a willing mind to give. They confirmed their willingness to give to the Apostle Paul a year earlier and now it was time to turn their willingness into the act of giving. Would their mind to give line up with their hands to give?

2 Corinthians 8:12 "For if there be first a willing mind, it is accepted according to that a man hath and not according to that he hath not."

This willing mind to give did not have a price tag attached to it. There was no set dollar amount to give. There was the accepted promise or vow to give and that was good enough. The fund collectors were not seeking to wring out as much as they possibly could from the church at Achaia. They were instead following up with the church at Achaia to fulfill their vow to give according to what they had to give and nothing more.

Deuteronomy 15:14b "...Give to him as the LORD your God has blessed you."

We are to give as the Lord has blessed us. What you don't have you surely can't give. Today we live in a society where borrowing money from banks, getting equity lines on homes, having multiple credit cards and lines of credit may falsely give us access to money that is not ours to give. Our willing mind shouldn't be used to put us into debt. A willing mind is accepted according to what we have, and not according to what we do not have. Going in debt to help the poor will only make us poorer. That is not God's intention for His children. God intends all believers to share in common what we have to share and if we all submit to this request none of us will ever lack or be in debt. To be in debt is to be required to submit to the authority of the debtor. God wants us to be the lenders and not the borrowers. He wants us to lend to the poor and owe no man anything except to love him.

There's a teaching that has spread to parts of the body of Christ to use their credit cards to give donations, i.e. to borrow money we can't pay back when the bill comes in within 30 days and accruing interest will cause us to be in debt. Is this the will of God? There are times you can give and there are times you need to be given to. No guilt required! No one should give so much that they put themselves in lack. No one should accept more than they need to get out of lack. In the body of Christ, out of love for our brothers and sisters, we don't gather too much, nor do we gather too little. (2 Corinthians 8:15) For each of us should have exactly what is needed. Those who have too much should share with those who have too little, so that those who have too little will have exactly what they need. Remember God says for those who give up what they have for the sake of the Kingdom of God, they will have much more on the earth and much more in eternity. You have no risk of loosing in the Kingdom of God when you follow Kingdom Principles of grace and truth in Jesus Christ. Even if you find yourself at some later date being the one in need you have the truth on your side. God promises when you give to the poor, He owes you Himself! (Proverbs 19:17) When believers participate in God's mindset of the Kingdom, having all things in common, those who have too much at the time you have too little, will supply your needs to bring you up out of lack.

Acts 2:44-45   "44 All the believers were together and had everything in common. 45 Selling their possessions and goods, they gave to anyone as he had need."

> Acts 4:32-35   "32 All the believers were one in heart and mind. No one claimed that any of his possessions was his own, but they shared everything they had. 33 With great power the apostles continued to testify to the resurrection of the Lord Jesus, and much grace was upon them all. 34 There were no needy persons among them. For from time to time those who owned lands or houses sold them, brought the money from the sales 35 and put it at the apostles' feet, and it was distributed to anyone as he had need."

Are we willing to operate rightly in the Kingdom of God by sharing all things in common with our fellow believers in Jesus Christ our LORD? This is the test for all of us. Are we willing to contribute individually or as a group to a common fund, administered by faithful believers with proven integrity to supply the needs of those believers who are in lack? Are we willing to love one another as we love ourselves?

> 1 John 3:17-20 "17 If anyone has material possessions and sees his brother in need but has no pity on him, how can the love of God be in him? 18 Dear children, let us not love with words or tongue but with actions and in truth. 19 This then is how we know that we belong to the truth, and how we set our hearts at rest in his presence."

Sharing Material blessings with those who have shared Their Spiritual Blessings

The church of Achaia is now at the place where they have to prove their love for God. They also have to prove their love for the Apostles and disciples to whom they made the promise. And last but not least, they have to prove their love for their brethren, the poor saints in Jerusalem. The church at Achaia are Gentile believer's in Jesus Christ taught by a Jewish Apostle, (Paul) and being asked of him to give to Jewish saints in Jerusalem. What???

God must have Something to Say about That!

Gentiles have shared in the Jew's (Israel) spiritual blessings. Gentiles owe it to the Jews to share with them their material blessings. (Romans 15:27b) What are these spiritual blessings Gentiles now share with Israel that should make all Gentiles pleased to make a contribution to the poor saints in Jerusalem? Why do Gentiles owe it to the Jews to share their material blessings with them? We will look at Romans 9:4-5, Ephesians 2:11-20 and Romans 11 to help answer these questions.

Romans 9:3-5 "3...my brothers, those of my own race, 4 the people of Israel. Theirs is:

- The adoption as sons,

- The divine glory,

- The covenants,

- The receiving of the law,

- The service of God,

- The promises;

- The patriarchs and from them is traced the human ancestry of Christ who is God over all, forever praised! Amen"

Who are the Israelites (Jews)? Are they everyone born in Israel or anyone who becomes a citizen of Israel? No! Israelites are the descendants of Abraham through his seed Isaac. Isaac is the father of Jacob whom God renamed Israel. These are the true Israelites because they are the chosen children of the promise. It is not the natural children who are God's children, but it is the children of the promise who are regarded as Abraham's offspring. The promise was given to Abraham, Isaac and Jacob, the Hebrew Patriarchs by God. Not all Israel is of Israel. (Romans 9:6) The descendants of Abraham through Ishmael are not the true Israelites because the promise was not given to them but to the seed that came forth from both Abraham and Sarah. The descendants of Isaac through Esau are also not the true Israel for the promise was given to Isaac's son Jacob. Out of all nations, Jacob (Israel) was selected to be God's treasured possession. Although the whole earth is the LORD's, the house of Jacob (Israel) is for God a kingdom of priests and a holy nation. (Exodus 19:3, 5, 6, Romans 9:6-16, Genesis 32:28)

Here lies a truth also for those who are members of churches of worship around the world. Not all who worship in the church is the true church. God told me once not to be disillusioned by any man. That includes men, women and children in the church. Within the walls of the church building and among those who call themselves the church are people who Jesus call wheat (the true church) and the tares (those planted by the evil one). Sometimes we can't tell the difference between the wheat and the tares at our places of worship but God can. He has chosen to keep them growing together because if He was to pluck out the tares some of the wheat would be plucked out also and God doesn't want that. (Matthew 13:24-30) God has promised never to allow the wheat to be plucked out of His hand. The blood of Jesus Christ guarantees this promise for the true church of Jesus Christ and the true Israel who are one man.

When we speak of Israel in this book, we are referring to the children of the guaranteed promise, Abraham, Isaac and Jacob (Israel) and their descendants after them. To them were granted the following spiritual blessings by God first. As we will see these same spiritual blessings were made available for Gentile believers in the Jewish Messiah, Jesus Christ: (Romans 1:16)

Adoption was first the Jews.

> Exodus 4:22 "… Then say to Pharaoh, 'This is what the LORD says: Israel is my firstborn son,"

> Jeremiah 31:9 "...because I am Israel's father, and Ephraim is my firstborn son."

Adoption is now also to the Gentile believers through Jesus Christ.

Ephesians 1:3-5 "3 Praise be to the God and Father of our Lord

> Jesus Christ, who has blessed us in the heavenly realms with every spiritual blessing in Christ. 4 For he chose us in him before the creation of the world to be holy and blameless in his sight. In love 5 he predestined us to be adopted as his sons through Jesus Christ, in accordance with his pleasure and will-"

The Glory pertains to the Jews first.

> Exodus 40:34-36 "34 Then the cloud covered the Tent of Meeting, and the glory of the LORD filled the tabernacle. 35 Moses could not enter the Tent of Meeting because the cloud had settled upon it, and the glory of the LORD filled the tabernacle. 36 In all the travels of the Israelites, whenever the cloud lifted from above the tabernacle, they would set out;"

> Luke 2:27-32 "27 When the parents brought in the child Jesus .… 28 Simeon took him in his arms and praised God, saying: 30 For my eyes have seen your salvation, 31 which you have prepared in the sight of all people, 32 a light for revelation to the Gentiles and for glory to your people Israel."

The Glory now also pertains to the Gentile believers through Jesus Christ.

Romans 8:17 "Now if we are children, then we are heirs-heirs of God and co-heirs with Christ, if indeed we share in his sufferings in order that we may also share in his glory."

The Covenants were given to the Jews first.

Genesis 17:2-8 "2 I will confirm my covenant between me and you and will greatly increase your numbers." 3 Abram fell facedown, and God said to him, 4 "As for me, this is my covenant with you: You will be the father of many nations. 5 No longer will you be called Abram; your name will be Abraham, for I have made you a father of many nations. 6 I will make you very fruitful; I will make nations of you, and kings will come from you. 7 I will establish my covenant as an everlasting covenant between me and you and your descendants after you for the generations to come, to be your God and the God of your descendants after you. 8 The whole land of Canaan, where you are now an alien, I will give as an everlasting possession to you and your descendants after you; and I will be their God."

Exodus 34:27-29 "27 Then the LORD said to Moses, "Write down these words, for in accordance with these words I have made a covenant with you and with Israel." 28 Moses was there with the LORD forty days and forty nights without eating bread or drinking water. And he wrote on the tablets the words of the covenant—the Ten Commandments."

Psalms 89:3-4 "3You said, "I have made a covenant with my chosen one, I have sworn to David my servant, 4'I will establish your line forever and make your throne firm through all generations.'"

Jeremiah 31:33-34 "33 This is the covenant I will make with the house of Israel after that time," declares the LORD. "I will put my law in their minds and write it on their hearts. I will be their God, and they will be my people. 34 No longer will a man teach his neighbor, or a man his brother, saying, 'Know the LORD,' because they will all know me, from the least of them to the greatest," declares the LORD. "For I will forgive their wickedness and will remember their sins no more." (see also Hebrews 8:6-10)

The covenants are now also given to the Gentiles.

Galatians 3:14 "He redeemed us in order that the blessing given to Abraham might come to the Gentiles through Christ Jesus, so that by faith we might receive the promise of the Spirit."

Acts 13:34 "And as concerning that he raised him up from the dead, now no more to return to corruption, he said on this wise, I will give you the sure mercies of David."

Hebrews 9:15 "For this reason Christ is the mediator of a new covenant, that those who are called may receive the promised eternal inheritance-now that he has died as a ransom to set them free from the sins..."

Hebrews 10:14-21 "14 because by one sacrifice he has made perfect forever those who are being made holy. 15 The Holy Spirit also testifies to us about this. First he says: 16 "This is the covenant I will make with them after that time, says the Lord. I will put my laws in their hearts, and I will write them on their minds." 17 Then he adds: "Their sins and lawless acts I will remember no more." 18 And where these have been forgiven, there is no longer any sacrifice for sin. 19 Therefore, brothers, since we have confidence to enter the Most Holy Place by the blood of Jesus, 20 by a new and living way opened for us through the curtain, that is, his body,"

God gave the Law to Israel first.

Psalms 147:19 "He has revealed his word to Jacob, his laws and decrees to Israel."

Malachi 4:4 "Remember the law of my servant Moses, the decrees and laws I gave him at Horeb for all Israel."

God has now also given His Law to the Gentiles.

Romans 8:1-4 "1 Therefore, there is now no condemnation for those who are in Christ Jesus, 2 because through Christ Jesus the law of the Spirit of life set me free from the law of sin and death. 3 For what the law was powerless to do in that it was weakened by the sinful nature, God did by sending his own Son in the likeness of sinful man to be a sin offering. And so he condemned sin in sinful man, 4 in order that the righteous requirements of the law might be fully met in us, who do not live according to the sinful nature but according to the Spirit."

The service of God was the honor of Israel to possess first.

Ezra 6:18 "And they installed the priests in their divisions and the Levites in their groups for the service of God at Jerusalem, according to what is written in the Book of Moses."

Exodus 12:25-27 "25 When you come to the land which the Lord will give you, as He has promised, you shall keep this service. 26 When your children shall say to you, What do you mean by this service? 27 You shall say, It is the sacrifice of the Lord's Passover," (AMP)

This honor to be of service to God is also now given to the Gentiles.

2 Corinthians 9:11-13 "11 You will be made rich in every way so that you can be generous on every occasion, and through us your generosity will result in thanksgiving to God. 12 This service that you perform is not only supplying the needs of God's people but is also overflowing in many expressions of thanks to God. 13 Because of the service by which you have proved yourselves, men will praise God for the obedience that accompanies your confession of the gospel of Christ, and for your generosity in sharing with them and with everyone else."

Ephesians 4:11-13 "11 It was he who gave some to be apostles, some to be prophets, some to be evangelists, and some to be pastors and teachers, 12 to prepare God's people for works of service, so that the body of Christ may be built up 13until we all reach unity in the faith and in the knowledge of the Son of God and become mature, attaining to the whole measure of the fullness of Christ."

The promises of God to participate in His divine nature were first given to the Jews.

Luke 1:68, 72-73 "68 Praise be to the Lord, the God of Israel, because he has come and has redeemed his people.72 to show mercy to our fathers and to remember his holy covenant, 73 the oath he swore to our father Abraham: "

The promises of God have also now been given to the Gentiles.

Ephesians 3:6 "...through the gospel the Gentiles are heirs together with Israel, members together of one body, and sharers together in the promise in Christ Jesus."

2 Peter 1:1-4 "To those who through the righteousness of our God and Savior Jesus Christ have received a faith as precious as ours: 3 His divine power has given us everything we need for life and godliness through our knowledge of him who called us by his own glory and goodness. 4 Through these he has given us his very great and precious promises, so that through them you may participate in the divine nature and escape the corruption in the world caused by evil desires."

As concerning the Patriarchs and human ancestry, Christ came as the seed of Abraham, Isaac and Jacob who is Israel.

Galatians 3:16-17 "16 The promises were spoken to Abraham and to his seed. The Scripture does not say "and to seeds," meaning many people, but "and to your seed," meaning one person, who is Christ."

As concerning the Spirit, Christ also came to the Gentiles

Romans 15:7-12 "7 Accept one another, then, just as Christ accepted you, in order to bring praise to God. 8 For I tell you that Christ has become a servant of the Jews on behalf of God's truth, to confirm the promises made to the patriarchs 9 so that the Gentiles may glorify God for his mercy, as it is written: Therefore I will praise you among the Gentiles; I will sing hymns to your name." 10 Again, it says, "Rejoice, O Gentiles, with his people."

11 And again, "Praise the Lord, all you Gentiles, and sing praises to him, all you peoples." 12 And again, Isaiah says, "The Root of Jesse will spring up, one who will arise to rule over the nations; the Gentiles will hope in him."

Just as Christ has accepted us, so are we to accept one another. It brings praise to God! The Jew accepting the Gentile believer brings praise to God. The Gentile believer accepting the Jew brings praise to God also. The Ethiopian Eunuch, an African Gentile "God fearer" accepted the teachings of Philip, a Jewish Apostle. Philip also accepted this first Gentile to believe in Jesus Christ* and baptized him as a sign of his new conversion. (Acts 8:26-39). Now they both had reason to rejoice and praise God and so they did. Today all nations are called to follow Jesus Christ. Now both Jews and Gentiles in Christ are God's treasured possession; His chosen children of promise. For God so loved the world that he gave his one and only Son, that whoever believes in him shall not perish but have eternal life. (John 3:16). Ephesians chapter 2 versus 11 through 20 emphasizes further this point.

Gentiles in the flesh were without Christ, being aliens from the commonwealth or citizenship of Israel, and strangers from the covenants of promise, having no hope, and without God in the world. But now in

Christ Jesus, Gentiles who sometimes were far off are now made nigh by the blood of Christ. Christ is our peace. He reconciled both Jew and Gentile into one body by the cross. Christ preached peace to those who were near (Jews covenanted with God) and to those who were far off (Gentiles without a covenant with God) and through Christ, both now have access by one Spirit to the Father. Now therefore Gentiles are no more strangers and foreigners but fellow citizens with God's people. We are members of God's household which is built on the foundation of the apostles and prophets with Christ as the Chief Cornerstone. (Ephesians 2:11-20 paraphrased)

Both Jews and Gentiles in Christ are now for God, a kingdom of priests and a holy nation. In 1 Peter 2:9,10, the audience is the Gentiles in Christ for whom God says, "9 But you are a chosen people, a royal priesthood, a holy nation, a people belonging to God, that you may declare the praises of him who called you out of darkness into his wonderful light. 10 Once you were not a people, but now you are the people of God; once you had not received mercy, but now you have received mercy."

Gentiles in Christ have obtained all the rights and privileges of citizenship in the commonwealth of Israel. This means everything common to Israel is now also common to or shared with Gentile Christians. All the wealth of Israel's adoption, glory, covenants, promises, service of God and their promised Messiah who is Jesus Christ, the son of the Living God is common to the new man in Christ made up of both Jew and Gentile. No longer two men but one man in Christ Jesus. No longer enemies or strangers. There is no more Jew or Gentile in the eyes of God; we are brothers and sisters and have all things in common, through our common Savior Jesus Christ. Salvation has come to the Gentiles!

The Olive Tree of Romans chapter 11 gives a visual depiction of this spiritual act of God assimilating the Gentiles into Israel's heritage. In this scripture, the Apostle Paul, apostle to the Gentiles, was addressing Gentiles comparing them to an olive tree that is wild by nature. In contrast, he referred to Israel as a cultivated olive tree. The apostle tells us in Romans 11:24, God engrafted the Gentile believers into the cultivated olive tree of Israel, thus combining both the natural branches who are Israel with the wild branches who are Gentiles into one cultivated olive tree. What was once Israel's alone is now extended to Gentile believers. Gentiles in the body of Christ share in the cultivated olive tree which is nourished and supported by God's holy root, the heritage of the Patriarch's Abraham, Isaac and Jacob whose name is Israel. The first fruit of Israel Abraham, Isaac and Jacob, is holy and therefore the whole batch or the whole olive tree of Israel is also holy.

By God's mercy Gentiles in Christ also partake of this holy root; the nourishing sap of God's promise to the Patriarchs of Israel.

> Romans 11:16-17 "16 If the part of the dough offered as first-fruits is holy, then the whole batch is holy; if the root is holy, so are the branches. 17 If some of the branches have been broken off, and you, though a wild olive shoot, have been grafted in among the others and now share in the nourishing sap from the olive root,"

> Romans 11:24-26 "24 After all, if you were cut out of an olive tree that is wild by nature, and contrary to nature were grafted into a cultivated olive tree, how much more readily will these, the natural branches, be grafted into their own olive tree! 25 I do not want you to be ignorant of this mystery, brothers, so that you may not be conceited: Israel has experienced a hardening in part until the full number of the Gentiles has come in. 26 And so all Israel will be saved "

All of Israel will be saved. (Romans 11:26) At this present time there is a remnant of Israel who has already received Jesus Christ Salvation according to the election of grace. The rest of Israel has experienced a hardening of the heart in part until the full number of the Gentiles has come into God's merciful Salvation, Jesus Christ. (Romans 11:25)

God has Flipped the Script Temporarily

God promised to prosper and keep Israel as long as they kept His commandments and did not turn to other gods. In Deuteronomy the 32nd chapter we see God speaking about rejection, unbelief, unfaithfulness, a turning away from Him, the only true God, to foreign gods. He continued to speak about desertion, abandonment and sacrifice to idols. God was describing Israel's betrayal and it made God angry and jealous. Jealous for Israel, His chosen people who He bought out of bondage from Egypt, set them apart from every other nation and prospered them. He kept Israel, provided for them in everyway, exalted them to the position of His children and committed to be their God. He wanted them back to worship Him alone. As His jealousy was kindled by this perverse generation, He said of Israel, "I will make them envious by those who are not a people; I will make them angry by a nation that has no understanding" Let's take a look:

> Deut 32:19-21 "The LORD saw this and rejected them because he was angered by his sons and daughters. 20 "I will hide my face from them," he said, "and see what their end will be; for they are a perverse generation, children who are unfaithful. 21 They made me jealous by what is no god and angered me with their worthless idols. I will make them envious by those who are not a people; I will make them angry by a nation that has no understanding. "

Gentiles were the nation without understanding and those who were not a people (i.e. who was not a Nation under the covenant of God). The salvation of Gentiles provokes Israel to jealousy turning them back to God. Yeshua is Jesus' name in Hebrew which means salvation. Salvation has come to the Gentiles in Jesus. Salvation for the Gentiles provides them with safety, deliverance, rescue and a defender. What Israel had for many generations', protection and provision from God, the same has been bought to Gentiles in Jesus Christ. Israel was blinded in part because of their unbelief. God hid His face from Israel making Israel in part like the Gentile nations surrounding them needing mercy. God's plan is to make Israel notice their lack of protection and provision and turn back to Him. God explains His will further in Deuteronomy 32:4, 36, 39 (paraphrased), He will have compassion on Israel when they find out their strength is gone and the foreign gods they worship are not able to help them or give them shelter. Then Israel will see there is no other God besides me and turn once again to their God; A faithful God who does no wrong, upright and just is he.

Israel Shall Be Saved

And so Israel shall be saved: As it is written, There shall come out of Zion the Deliverer, and shall turn away ungodliness from Jacob (Israel): For this is my covenant unto them, when I shall take away their sins. (Romans 11:26-27)

The same mercy God showed the Gentiles in their unbelief is the same mercy He will show to Israel in their unbelief when the full number of Gentiles has been bought into the Kingdom of Jesus Christ. He has promised to have mercy on all. (Romans 11:32). God flipped the script for a time. The LORD our God is one! There is no other God besides Him; None before and none after Him. The same God who bought Salvation to Israel by His mighty hand, delivering them from the bondage of Egypt is the same God who bought salvation to the Gentiles, delivering them from the bondage of sin. He is also the same God who has and will have mercy on Israel delivering them from the sin of unbelief. Israel has not been replaced. God forbid!

God will gather the lost sheep of Israel to Himself for God's gift and his call of Israel is irrevocable. It can not be taken away or removed. (Romans 11:29). Praise is to God! Our great lesson here is: once you are chosen by God and sealed by His everlasting covenant, God will never leave or forsake you or His everlasting covenant. Yes, in part the Jews heart has been hardened because of their unbelief and many of the branches were cutoff their olive tree, but in God's mercy and because of His promise to never break His covenant, the Jews who believe will be engrafted back again onto the cultivated olive tree. Ungodliness or the sin of unbelief will be taken away from Israel, for this is God's Covenant with Israel. (Romans 11:23) See there is no need to divide the body of Christ from the Jew, Jesus doesn't. He died to make us one man, He rose to nourish one olive tree, and He was ascended to be one Lord over all.

God has a one mind focus. Unity in the Body of Christ is God's mindset. Let us join Him. We are to have this same mind of Christ. God has bound himself by His word and His covenant, He said in Psalms 89:34, "I will not violate my covenant or alter what my lips have uttered."

Nor has God forgotten about His covenant with Israel. God is not a covenant breaker! It is through the fall of Israel that Salvation has come to the Gentiles to provoke the Jews to jealousy. (Romans 11:11) Israel's fall and their exclusion from the benefits of Salvation in part, bought the riches of God's glory to the Gentiles world. And even more

* Keener, Craig S. "The IVP Bible Background Commentary: New Testament" (Intervarsity Press: Downers Grove, Illinois, 1993) 345.

so, when Israel's blindness is removed and they arise having admission to the benefits of Salvation again. After God's set time, then they will bring nothing short of life from the dead! (Romans 11:15, Amplified, paraphrased)

Hallelujah! The one and only God; The King and High Priest, has blessed all the nations of the earth fulfilling the promises given to David and the patriarchs, Abraham, Isaac and Jacob. Therefore, Gentiles are blessed because of the inheritance given to the Jews first. So am I saying many Gentile believers have it backwards? Yes, that's exactly what I am saying.

We have it backwards!

For years I've heard Gentile believers in Christ say, we have to reach the Jews to bring them into the new covenant because they are in the old covenant which has been done away with. I've also heard we need to bring the Jews to the Gentile savior Jesus Christ and they will live and not die. The truth is the new covenant was given to the Jews first. Jesus Christ is the Messiah of the Jews first and was born out of the lineage of Abraham, Isaac, Jacob and David all of whom are Jews. The first apostles of Christ were Jews. They took the revelation of the gospel of Jesus Christ to the Gentiles and that's how Gentile believers even know about Christ, from the Jews. (Ephesians 3:7-9) The church has not replaced Israel as the chosen people of God. The church built by Jesus Christ on the foundation of revelation given us from heaven is both for the Jew and the Gentile. There are not two Kingdoms of God. There is only one Kingdom of God, governed by His Son Jesus Christ. There is one nation, one Lord, and one faith. Separation is of man not of God. The Gentiles have come into the revelation given unto Israel first and not the opposite. Israel doesn't need a new revelation from Gentile believers about the Messiah, they just need to submit to God and receive of their Messiah whom the Father has already sent them. Many Jews have already done so, Praise God. Many Gentiles have believed the message of the Jewish Messiah born in Bethlehem and Savior of the world, Jesus Christ. Jesus was born to be a light for revelation to the Gentiles and to bring glory to Israel, the receiver, keeper and distributor of God's Word. Everything God spoke to Israel came true and it was proven in the Messiah, to the glory of Israel. Jesus Christ: a light for revelation to the Gentiles and for glory to your people Israel." (Luke 2:32)

Gentiles have received of the spiritual blessings of Israel. Gentile's the world over should be delighted and pleased to share our material wealth with the poor saints in Jerusalem and beyond. Gentiles owe a great debt of gratitude to Israel for spreading the revelation of the gospel of Jesus Christ given to them. They risked persecution, excommunication, jail, and death to preach God's word and witness the gospel of faith to the Gentiles in the uttermost parts of the earth. Do Gentiles owe Israel? You bet! As a Gentile believer myself, I am pleased to contribute to the needs of Israel and I am delighted to use my material wealth to help remove the financial lack of my brothers and sisters in Christ, the Jews. Praise God!

1 Chronicles 29:9-14

9 The people rejoiced at the willing response of their leaders, for they had given freely and wholeheartedly to the LORD.

David the king also rejoiced greatly.

10 David praised the LORD in the presence of the whole assembly, saying,

"Praise be to you, O LORD,

God of our father Israel,

from everlasting to everlasting.

11 Yours, O LORD, is the greatness and the power

and the glory and the majesty and the splendor,

for everything in heaven and earth is yours.

Yours, O LORD, is the kingdom;

you are exalted as head over all.

12 Wealth and honor come from you;

you are the ruler of all things.

In your hands are strength and power

to exalt and give strength to all.

13 Now, our God, we give you thanks,

and praise your glorious name.

14 "But who am I, and who are my people, that we should be able to give as generously as this? Everything comes from you, and we have given you only what comes from your hand.

Kingdom Teaching and Instructions to Excel in the Grace of Giving

Common Wealth

Faith-Wealth to Share and Care for God's People

To share wealth, we have to gain wealth. Wealth can be gained on the earth in two ways; by the strength of our hands or by the power and strength of God. The world has proven to us over and over again that the wicked can amass wealth thus we know wealth is not always a sign of God's favor. We know it is possible to gain wealth by the power of our hands but wealth without righteousness is worthless. (Psalms 37:16, 17)

> Proverbs 11:4-8 "4 Wealth is worthless in the day of wrath, but righteousness delivers from death. 5 The righteousness of the blameless makes a straight way for them, but the wicked are brought down by their own wickedness. 6 The righteousness of the upright delivers them, but the unfaithful are trapped by evil desires. 7 When a wicked man dies, his hope perishes; all he expected from his power comes to nothing. 8 The righteous man is rescued from trouble, and it comes on the wicked instead."

There is no eternal gain in gathering wealth amassed by sheer human power. It temporarily satisfies and can only be enjoyed while you have it or while you are alive to spend it. Once it's gone or you're gone, your wealth's value to you is also gone. The money you gain today can be lost tomorrow. The wealth you achieve today and store up for tomorrow may be left for another to use. (Proverbs 28:8) So what lasting effects is there in gaining wealth by the power and struggle of your hands if there is no guarantee the fruit of your labor will last pass tomorrow or your lifetime? What hope does wealth gained by the power of your hands provide for you? Hope in wealth has no satisfying end.

Ecclesiastes 5:10 "Whoever loves money never has money enough; whoever loves wealth is never satisfied with his income. This too is meaningless "

We are not to put our hope in wealth but we are to put our hope in God. Believers, we are to not look to the things of the earth to fulfill us, for they will grow old, wear out, break, die out, go from treasure to trash, go out of style, and/or get lost or stolen. Wealth gained is never to become a god in our lives. Money and Material possessions should never be more highly valued than people. Money and possessions are never to rule our decisions. Money for the sake of gaining money or money for the sake of hoarding money should never be our motivation for increasing our wealth. Our monetary gain should be motivated by God's word and nothing else. Our true need can't be purchased, eaten or withdrawn from a bank. God has designed us to need bigger than ourselves and to stretch beyond ourselves to depend on Him and others. Money, food, clothing, material possessions gained by human strength provide limited satisfaction and comfort.

Ecclesiastes 5:11 "As goods increase, so do those who consume them. And what benefit are they to the owner except to feast his eyes on them?"

God, the creator of heaven and earth, supplies us with 100% of what we need every day of our earthly life and our eternal life. God's gift of His Son and our Savior and Lord, Jesus Christ has given us access to All Spiritual Gifts in the Heavenly realm. (Ephesians 1: 3) We are no longer limited to the things of the earthly realm alone. God has expanded our reach and spreads open our borders to intimately commune with Him and receive of His provisions for all our need and the needs of others.

Romans 8:32 "He who did not spare his own Son, but gave him up for us all—how will he not also, along with him, graciously give us all things?"

We have been given the gift of "all things" through the Spirit without limit in Christ. Our limits are set only by our faith in, trust in, confidence in, and our belief in our one and only true and living God. Take the limits off your faith and let God feed you, provide for you and love you with an everlasting love where He graciously gives us all things in Christ Jesus.

John 3:34 "For the one whom God has sent speaks the words of God, for God gives the Spirit without limit. "

Wealth gained by sheer human power has its limits. But wealth gained by God's power is unlimited in its reach. God's wealth is commonwealth. Commonwealth is a compound word. Common means communion or fellowship expressing the idea of sharing as in sharing together as one. Wealth means an abundance of possessions. When we put these two words together commonwealth means an abundance of possessions that are shared together in a community or fellowship. We live under a commonwealth system in the Kingdom of God. God's commonwealth economic system succeeds when we are faithful stewards of God's faith-wealth. When we are not faithful stewards of God's faith-wealth given us to prosper the King's Kingdom and care for the needs of the King's children, the commonwealth plan is not fully realized. Thank God He is faithful when we are faithless. God is our provider even beyond our unfaithfulness and He still is the one who gives us the ability to produce wealth to confirm his covenant which He will not break.

> Deuteronomy 8:17-18 "17 You may say to yourself, "My power and the strength of my hands have produced this wealth for me." 18 But remember the LORD your God, for it is he who gives you the ability to produce wealth, and so confirms his covenant, which he swore to your forefathers, as it is today."

God has one thing in mind in giving us the ability to produce wealth that is to fulfill His covenant promises of provision He made to His people. Wealth produced by the power and strength of God has a far greater purpose than our own personal achievement, satisfaction or security. The wealth God produces through us confirms his word which is never void of power. God intends for us to take the wealth He produces and mix it with faith in His word to fulfill His covenant of provision to love and care for His children.

Wealth to Care for a Nation

Covenanted by God

Faithful in His Love for Us

From the Garden of Eden to the Garden of Gethsemane; from the staff of Moses to the Cross of Christ; from Jesus dwelling with us on earth to the Holy Spirit dwelling with us in our eternal dwellings, God has lavished His love on us. He has no intention to stop.

God has covenanted to love those who follow Him to a thousand generations.

Deuteronomy 7:9 "Know therefore that the LORD your God is God; he is the faithful God, keeping his covenant of love to a thousand generations of those who love him and keep his commands."

God is faithful to His covenants and He will never break them.

Psalms 89:34 "I will not violate my covenant or alter what my lips have uttered."

God remembers His covenants forever.

Psalms 105:8-10 "8 He remembers his covenant forever, the word he commanded, for a thousand generations, 9 the covenant he made with Abraham, the oath he swore to Isaac. 10 He confirmed it to Jacob as a decree, to Israel as an everlasting covenant:"

God ordains His redemption and His covenant forever.

Psalms 111:9 "He provided redemption for his people; he ordained his covenant forever— holy and awesome is his name."

Producing wealth to provide for God's Kingdom of priests and kings is a covenantal promise of God's. With God there is to be ever enduring wealth and prosperity. In righteousness and justice He bestows wealth and riches on His people who love Him. By God's power and strength He is able to make our treasuries, on earth and in heaven, full.

Proverbs 8:18-21 "18 With me are riches and honor, enduring wealth and prosperity. 19 My fruit is better than fine gold; what I yield surpasses choice silver. 20 I walk in the way of righteousness, along the paths of justice, 21 bestowing wealth on those who love me and making their treasuries full."

Wealth comes from God who is the ruler of all things. (1 Chronicles 29:12). Sharing the faith-wealth produced in the Kingdom of God is the necessary response to any priest or king of the Kingdom who is in poverty. This is the LORD's justice. Psalm 140:12 "I know that the LORD secures justice for the poor and upholds the cause of the needy."

To faithfully operate in the system of commonwealth, God's people will have to use God's principles of giving and receiving. Kingdom Teaching and Instructions that enables us to Excel in the Grace of Giving and Receiving

The Apostle Paul, in 2 Corinthians chapter 9, believes the church at Achaia will mix the wealth God produced in them with faith in God's word to uphold the cause of the poor securing justice for them. God gave the church at Achaia wealth and He opened up a redistribution of wealth opportunity in the body of Christ for them to participate. God made them aware that the saints in Jerusalem were poor and in need of their financial help. To facilitate the redistribution of wealth from the wealthy to the poor, God rose up proven, faithful and godly administrators to organize and collect the wealth and distribute the contributions. God showers His people with grace to fulfill His covenant of love by providing us with wealth to share.

To help the church at Achaia excel in the grace of giving, Paul sent Titus and the other disciples in Christ to encourage them to finish the arrangements for the generous gift promised. The letter written to this church reveals five of God's Kingdom teachings and instructions on how to excel in the grace of giving and receiving. They are:

1. Give to the poor as God commands: Do justice and have mercy on the needy.

2.   Give with a heart of joy and purpose: God loves a cheerful giver.

3.   The Grace of God enables us to give and receive: When you give God is able to make all grace abound to you, so that in all things, at all times, having all that you need, you will abound in every good work.

4.   Sow in righteousness and your righteousness will be forever remembered by God. He increases your seed, multiplies your harvest and causes the fruits of your righteousness to abound. The righteous "sower" is made rich in every way so that they can be generous on every occasion.

5.   Giving is a service of God. Service to the saints brings thanksgiving to God.

God is glorified when we give because we show the poor saints we are willing to submit to our confession of the gospel of Jesus Christ.

Grace will be the force of God that enables the Church at Achaia to redistribute their faith-wealth to the needy. The power of God's love in this church would be the tie that binds both poor and wealthy together as one. Grace must be exercised and love must be given out. The administrators of the collection knew the church at Achaia had to mature to exercise grace in giving and love in sharing generously and willingly. Therefore grace was given to the apostle and teachers to mature the saints of God at Achaia. To each, grace is given as Christ apportions it.

Apostles and teachers are given to the body of Christ to prepare God's people for works of service so that believers may be built up, united in faith and in the knowledge of Jesus Christ. We are matured as saints by the truth of God and nothing else. We grow up in the teaching of the truth under the head whom is Christ. It is in Christ that the whole body is joined together, growing and building itself in love, as each part does its work. (Ephesians 4:7-16) Speaking the truth in love enables apostles, teachers, pastors, prophets, evangelist and disciples to demolish arguments and every pretension that sets itself up against the knowledge of God, taking every thought and making it obedient to Christ. (2 Corinthians10:5)

Wow! The power of truth and the power of love strip out of us falseness and deceitfulness. The power of truth in love exalts us to obedience in Christ. The Church at Achaia was being taught the truth. They were faced with the choice to be obedient or disobedient to the teaching and instructions of God that explain how they can excel at the grace of giving to the poor.

Join me on the journey of discovering the truth uncovered in 2 Corinthians chapter 9 that God wants all of us to know about giving and receiving.

2 Corinthians 9:3-5

"3 But I am sending the brothers in order that our boasting about you in this matter should not prove hollow, but that you may be ready, as I said you would be. 4 For if any Macedonians come with me and find you unprepared, we-not to say anything about you-would be ashamed of having been so confident. 5 So I thought it necessary to urge the brothers to visit you in advance and finish the arrangements for the generous gift you had promised.

Attaining Justice and Mercy for the Poor, Needy and Lacking

Making our righteousness shine!

Proverbs 29:7 "The righteous care about justice for the poor, but the wicked have no such concern."

Doing justice for the poor is a characteristic of the righteous. Not caring about the poor is a characteristic of the wicked.

The Church at Achaia was faced with the choice of whether or not to execute justice for the needy and have mercy on the poor. Would they remember the words given by the Lord Jesus himself in Acts 20:35b: 'It is more blessed to give than to receive'? Would they allow God to prove Himself in this truth or would they like many in the church today only see themselves blessed when they receive a raise, land, a home, a car, a new church building, a new job, a spouse, money, etc.; looking to the material possession or money to prove they are blessed. The words Jesus speaks are Spirit and they are Life. Let us have faith that the word of God that is unseen, in the Spirit realm is already working in the Physical realm bringing life where it's needed. Faith is the evidence of things not seen, not of things seen. If we focus on what is seen only, we miss the greater blessing. Let God prove to us it is always more blessed to give than to receive.

We are not to forget to do well and to share with others. God says, with such sacrifices He is pleased. (Hebrews 13:16) God takes pleasure in our giving. He goes beyond encouraging us to give to commanding us to give.

God commands that we give to the poor and needy!

Deuteronomy 15:11 "There will always be poor people in the land. Therefore I command you to be openhanded toward your brothers and toward the poor and needy in your land."

We are not to be hard of heart or tightfisted when one of our brothers or sisters is in need. We are to be openhanded, generous and of a willing heart; freely giving him and her whatever they need. (Deuteronomy 15:7, 8) It is God's people who supply the plenty that will overcome the lack of any and all saints in need. The saints take care of the saints in the Kingdom of God. God doesn't intend for there to be any poor among the saints, for He richly blesses us to be able to fully take care of all those in the kingdom.

Deuteronomy 15:4 "However, there should be no poor among you, for in the land the LORD your God is giving you to possess as your inheritance, he will richly bless you,"

> James 2:14-17 "14 What good is it, my brothers, if a man claims to have faith but has no deeds? Can such faith save him? 15 Suppose a brother or sister is without clothes and daily food. 16 If one of you says to him, "Go, I wish you well; keep warm and well fed," but does nothing about his physical needs, what good is it? 17 In the same way, faith by itself, if it is not accompanied by action, is dead."

When we give to the poor we honor God. When we don't give to the poor and oppress them or allow their oppression we show contempt for God.

Proverbs 14:31 "He who oppresses the poor shows contempt for their Maker, but whoever is kind to the needy honors God."

God goes as far as to say if we ignore the poor, He will ignore us.

Proverbs 21:13 "If a man shuts his ears to the cry of the poor, he too will cry out and not be answered"

On the other hand, when we share with the poor, God counts us as generous and declare us blessed. We will lack nothing.

Proverbs 28:27 "He who gives to the poor will lack nothing, but he who closes his eyes to them receives many curses."

God never forsakes the hungry or the thirsty and neither should we.

Isaiah 41:17   "The poor and needy search for water, but there is none; their tongues are parched with thirst. But I the LORD will answer them; I, the God of Israel, will not forsake them."

1 John 3:17 "If anyone has material possessions and sees his brother in need but has no pity on him, how can the love of God be in him? "

We are not only to care for strangers locally and overseas but we are to provide for the needs of our own flesh and blood that is poor. We should not turn away our family if they are in need.

Isaiah 58:7   "Is it not to share your food with the hungry and to provide the poor wanderer with shelter— when you see the naked, to clothe him, and not to turn away from your own flesh and blood?"

1 Timothy 5:8   "If anyone does not provide for his relatives, and especially for his immediate family, he has denied the faith and is worse than an unbeliever. "

God intends for His people to do judgment and justice. Helping the poor and needy by defending their cause, judging their cause worthy and pleading their case is what God intends for us to do.

Jeremiah 22:15-16 ....He did what was right and just, so all went well with him. 16 He defended the cause of the poor and needy, and so all went well. Is that not what it means to know me?" declares the LORD.

God ask a question in Jeremiah 22:16: "was not this to know me?" To know God is to do judgment and justice on earth by taking up the cause of the poor and needy. To know God is know the dept of His heart and what He wants us to do for it to go well with us. To know God means we must have an intimate relationship. This phrase emphasizes the depth of the relationship we are to have with Him. When we take the time to know and understand God we discover God exercises kindness, justice and righteousness on earth. It is in these that the LORD is delighted. (Jeremiah 9:24) Those who know God persevere to acknowledge God in all of their ways and trust God in all they do. To know God is to keep His word. When we know God, truly know Him, our actions follow the knowledge of God we have. We know we have come to know God if we obey His commands. (1 John 2:3-4) God commands us to give to the poor and needy! When we obey this command it confirms we have come to know God and it will be well with us.

On the other hand if we do not obey the command of the Lord to give to the poor and needy it will not go well with us. Ezekiel chapter 16 tells us of why Sodom was destroyed. The citizens of Sodom did many acts of evil but God specifically mentions that they did not help the poor and needy. God said Sodom was unconcerned about the poor and needy. He called this sin. Yes, not helping the poor and needy when it is within your ability to help is sinful. It's being on the side of evil to not help the poor when you have the ability to help. Many in Sodom had plenty and they chose to use their plenty for their own personal pleasures and ignore their brethren who had no food, shelter, clothes, who were sick and imprisoned. God punished them for their neglect of the poor and needy.

Ezekiel 16:49, "'Now this was the sin of your sister Sodom: She and her daughters were arrogant, overfed and unconcerned; they did not help the poor and needy.'"

When we close our eyes to the need of the poor, God says many a curse will come upon us. "….It is a curse to hide your eyes from the poor (Proverbs 28:27). It is not a curse to be poor as some would say. But curses come upon us when we are able to but choose not to supply the need of the poor. Jesus became poor that we might become rich.

Many don't realize God's plan for the poor. Many see the poor and look down on them or feel sorry for them whether they choose to help or not. God doesn't look at the poor and the needy this way and he doesn't want us to either. God wants us to see the poor as an opportunity in front of us when we become aware of someone who is in need. It's an opportunity for us to be a blessing. When Gentile believers came into the new covenant by the blood and flesh of Jesus Christ we became Abraham's seed also. (Galatians 3:7-9) All under the covenant of Abraham are blessed to be a blessing. Our work on this earth is to be a blessing to all nations who will in return call us blessed. When we as God's representatives are called blessed, that in turn brings glory to God because He is recognized as the God of the blessed. God has a purpose for us giving to the poor and that is God's kindness brings man to repentance. (Romans 2:4) Forgiveness and Salvation can come to the house of the poor through our obedience of giving and receiving!

The poor is defined as one needing daily necessities; to become indigent. Indigent means poor or destitute; being poor enough to need help from others. Jesus became poor. (2 Corinthians 8:9). How many of us viewed Jesus as poor? Jesus became poor for the blessing opportunity to make us rich. How many of us incorrectly view being poor as a curse and not as an opportunity to be a blessing. Jesus gave up His heavenly glory and humbled Himself having no reputation, becoming a human being and a servant for us.

> Philippians 2:5-8 "5 Your attitude should be the same as that of Christ Jesus: 6 Who, being in very nature God, did not consider equality with God something to be grasped, 7 but made himself nothing, taking the very nature of a servant, being made in human likeness. 8 And being found in appearance as a man, he humbled himself and became obedient to death- even death on a cross!

Some Bible interpretations say Jesus made himself "nothing". Nothing is a pretty tough word to swallow especially when the word goes on to say He was made in the likeness of men. Does that mean men are nothing? By no means! Men were created by God, and as servants of God we are in need of God whether we are aware of it or not. Jesus, who came from the Father gave up His glorified rights and privileges and took on a human body so that He could bless us with grace and truth (John 1:14). Jesus' poverty was reflected in His absolute need of the Father to direct Him in words and visions. Jesus only did what the Father showed Him and only said what the Father told Him to say. (John 5:19, 8:28) The Father and His son Jesus Christ are one. The son of man was in need of the LORD's Holy Spirit to anoint Him and lead Him to accomplish all the commands of God without sin. Jesus was anointed to preach good news to the poor. (Luke 4:18) He preached to those who were destitute of good news and needed to know that the Kingdom of Heaven was near. Being poor is not to be looked upon with pity or indignation, but rather looked at with a humble mind that sees God's vision to supply their need fully. This is no different than when God supplied our need for salvation when we were poor in spirit.

God's own example of the Son of God becoming poor, meaning Jesus was in need of the Father fully while He was on earth shows God doesn't despise the poor. God loves the poor. God desires that the poor be filled and moved out of poverty as Christ did by obedience to the Father. (Philippians 2: 8-11) Every human being is nothing and can do nothing without God. We will always be found wanting and needy without God. He is faithful to supply our need. Will we be faithful to supply the needs of others as we are able? Like Christ we are to become obedient to God in every way saying only what God speaks and doing only what God shows us. Will you be humbled imitating Christ and allowing the Holy Spirit to bring you into the direct reflected image of Christ? Letting the same mind that is in Christ be in you. The result is awesome, together we become a blessing. Fulfilling the covenant, we are blessed to be a blessing, even to all the nations of the earth.

Again, being poor is not a curse! Many point to Deuteronomy chapter 28 as the blessing and curses chapter pulling several verses out of context and proclaiming that being poor is a curse. God proclaimed to the nation of Israel if they obey His commandments they will be blessed and if they disobeyed His commandments and forsake His ways and do not revere His glorious and awesome name they will be cursed. To forsake God is to leave God or to refuse to submit to His authority. God was not talking to any individual then or now, He was speaking to a nation of people. Financial poverty for any individual is not a curse. It is tough, disheartening, stressful and sometimes depressing to be poor but not a curse. God saw Israel as one whole nation and not as individuals. God sees the body of Christ and all those destined to inherit the new covenant as one whole Kingdom and not individuals. It is the disobedience of the nation of Israel that would cause God's curses according to Deuteronomy chapter 28 to come upon their bodies, their land and/or their possessions. The lack of financial resources or a generation to generation pattern of financial lack should not necessarily be interpreted as someone or a family being under the curse of God. God's curses were meant to destroy or abandon the nations land, resources and/or lives. God was and is extremely tolerant of the disobedience of His chosen people and lavishes great mercy and grace to turn His chosen back to Him long before the curse of God would come upon the nation. It is a great burden and Biblically incorrect to put upon any individual member of the body of Christ a thought or title of being cursed in   their finances. One who is in lack can come out of lack not because they are delivered from a curse but because they are loved by God and loved by their neighbor. The poor saints in Jerusalem were not considered to be cursed but in need of help in 2 Corinthians chapter 9.

God is clear in the Bible; He doesn't want His people poor.

> Deuteronomy 15:4-6   "However, there should be no poor among you, for in the land the LORD your God is giving you to possess as your inheritance, he will richly bless you, 5 if only you fully obey the LORD your God and are careful to follow all these commands I am giving you today. 6 For the LORD your God will bless you as he has promised, and you will lend to many nations but will borrow from none. You will rule over many nations but none will rule over you."

There will always be poor people in the land for believers to help. God commands us to give to them especially to the family of believers.

Deuteronomy 15:11   "There will always be poor people in the land. Therefore I command you to be openhanded toward your brothers and toward the poor and needy in your land."

Therefore out of obedience to God, believers will always be giving to the poor.

Galatians 6:9-10 "Let us not become weary in doing good, for at the proper time we will reap a harvest if we do not give up. Therefore, as we have opportunity, let us do good to all people, especially to those who belong to the family of believers."

1 Chronicles 28:9

"…….. acknowledge the God of your father,

and serve him with wholehearted devotion and

with a willing mind,

for the LORD searches every heart and

understands every motive behind the thoughts."

Give as You Purpose with Your Heart

God loves a cheerful giver.

God takes pleasure in those whose heart is motivated out of pure joy to give. Our attitude toward giving and receiving or sowing and reaping makes all the difference in the world to God. Paul is telling the church at Achaia to remember this reality. How we think about giving will translate into how and what we give.

Deuteronomy 15:10 "Give generously to him and do so without a grudging heart; then because of this the LORD your God will bless you in all your work and in everything you put your hand to."

God says in Deuteronomy 15:10, we are to give generously and to do so without a grudging or stingy heart. This scripture provides the key to how to give. We are to be willing and generous in our giving! When we give willingly and generously, God promises to bless us in all our work and in everything we put our hands to. You can't get a better guarantee than that. There is nothing you won't be prosperous in when you follow God's word to be generous to those in need and have a heart that is joyous in your giving.

> 2 Corinthians 9:6, 7 "6[Remember] this: he who sows sparingly and grudgingly will also reap sparingly and grudgingly, and he who sows generously [that blessings may come to someone] will also reap generously and with blessings. Let each one [give] as he has made up his own mind and purposed in his heart, not reluctantly or sorrowfully or under compulsion, for God loves (He takes pleasure in, prizes above other things, and is unwilling to abandon or to do without) a cheerful (joyous, "prompt to do it") giver [whose heart is in his giving]." AMP

When we give sparingly we have an attitude that does not please God. To give sparingly doesn't mean we give a little because we have a little, it means we give a little because we are stingy. The stingy person has more to give but chooses to keep it for themselves instead of giving more out of their overflow to those who are in need. This verse doesn't just say the one who gives sparingly reaps sparingly. 2 Corinthians chapter 9 verse 6 goes further and says the one who gives sparingly and grudgingly also reaps sparingly and grudgingly. To give grudgingly means to give with sorrow or to give with a heavy and unwilling heart. People who give very little as compared to what they could give or what little they do give, they give reluctantly, unwillingly and only because they feel for some reason they have to; these people will reap sparingly and grudgingly. Many people have little to give because they have little overflow but they give their little cheerfully. These people are not who Paul was speaking about regarding those who will reap sparingly and grudgingly. Others may have a lot of overflow and they give generously (i.e. above and beyond, unselfishly and with a kind and warm heart). Behind giving generously and giving sparingly/grudgingly is an attitude or motivation that precedes our action of giving. An unselfish and loving heart will cause us to give generously whether we have a little to give or a lot to give. A selfish and unwilling heart will cause us to give reluctantly if we are rich, poor or somewhere in between. Remember this, God loves a cheerful giver. God "prizes above other things" a joyous giver whose heart is in his giving. God will not abandon a giver who is cheerful.

Please understand God is not trying to get anything out of us that we are not willing to cheerfully give. Whatever Alms we choose to give, God wants us to be motivated by love and joy. Some might try to oversimplify verse 6 of 2 Corinthians chapter 9 by saying the more we give, the more we receive. But that would then make giving and receiving based solely on the amount of our wealth. It would seem then the prosperity of the Bible would be stacked against those who have little and in favor of those who have much. Not So! It's not the quantity of the giving, we know this to be true by the story of the widows mite in Luke 21:2-3, and the story of the widow of Zarephath in 1 Kings 17:7-16; it's the heart of the giver that gets God's attention and causes Him to respond by providing a harvest. Just because someone is a millionaire and they're able to give $100,000.00 and we are a "hundred-aire" and we're only able to give $10.00, doesn't mean the millionaire will be abundantly more blessed than the "hundred-aire". Why is this? Our return is not based on money in, money out but it is based on what our loving, righteous and joyous heart displays in our giving.

What ever we purposed in our heart, give it according to the foundation of love poured into us by the power of the Holy Spirit (Romans 5: 5) Give it cheerfully for this is what God loves. When we discover what God loves we should want to do it, we should want to say it and we should want to be apart of it.

Isn't it exciting to know how simple it is to line up with what God loves and please God with our giving? God loves a cheerful giver. Cheerful means joyous, merry, prompt in your response or willing. Cheerful should not be confused with happy which is an emotional response. One minute we can be happy based on a particular circumstance in our life and another moment the happiness ceases. Sowing seed is not based on our emotions. Cheerfully sowing is the same as sowing with a heart full of joy. But where does this joy come from? It doesn't come as a result of our circumstances or our current situations. Joy is not here one moment and gone the next. Joy is the fruit of the Spirit, a gift from the Holy Spirit to us and in us. (Galatians 5:22) We have the joy of the Lord in us; Christ in us our hope of glory has taken up residence in the temple of every believer.

John 17:13 "I am coming to you now, but I say these things while I am still in the world, so that they may have the full measure of my joy within them."

The full measure of Jesus' joy was within the disciples and is within all who believe also. The joy of the Lord is our strength. The joy of the Lord fulfilled in us strengthens us to give beyond our current circumstances or situations. Joy brings confidence in God's word to do what God loves. This joy helps us see beyond the beginning, seed sowing to seeing the end result, receiving the harvest. You see, Joy takes our heart out of worry or anxiousness about our future. The Joy of the Lord in us shows us our future and it's better than our present when we obey God and choose to please Him. God takes pleasure in the joyful (cheerful) heart of a giver. This joy that we have the world didn't give it to us and the world can't take it away! Let's allow Jesus' joy to motivate us into applying God's principles to obtain the abundant future He has planned for us.

It was the Joy set before our Lord Jesus Christ that enabled Him to endure the cross.

Hebrews 12:2 "Let us fix our eyes on Jesus, the author and perfecter of our faith, who for the joy set before him endured the cross, scorning its shame, and sat down at the right hand of the throne of God."

The joy of what would happen in the future motivated Jesus to be obedient in the present. The joy of bringing salvation, redemption, and victory over Satan to mankind; the joy of returning again to the glory of heaven and completing His work on earth; the joy of blessing mankind by His finished work on the cross reconciling the world back to Himself motivated Jesus with joy to get to the other side of the cross. The power of Jesus' joy is the same joy in us. The joy in our hearts burst with thanksgiving for our new abundant life sealed in the power of the Holy Spirit by Jesus' blood. The joy in our hearts motivates us to love God the same way Christ love motivated Him. Are you as joyful as Jesus is about your redemption, about your salvation and your eternal life? Do you see the future? Are you convinced of your abundant life to the extent that you will complete the service God has for you to do? Joy motivates us to go beyond our feelings. We're motivated to act out of what's in our hearts because of the joy that is set before us!

We give because we love God. We don't have to be pressured into giving. We should purpose in our heart what to give; not as other people expect, but as our heart is directing us to give.

Lessons of a Purposeful Heart

> Hebrews 4:12-13 "12 For the word of God is living and active. Sharper than any double-edged sword, it penetrates even to dividing soul and spirit, joints and marrow; it judges the thoughts and attitudes of the heart. 13 Nothing in all creation is hidden from God's sight. Everything is uncovered and laid bare before the eyes of him to whom we must give account."

God knows the condition of our heart when we sow into the lives of others. Our heart reveals our true intentions and our deepest thoughts. He can see what's in our heart, past, present and future. Our heart cannot lie! It's an open book to the Lord; nothing can be hidden from Him. Our heart will give account of our life to God. He is the one we must give account. The Word of God judges the thoughts and attitudes of the heart. Our harvest reaped will be a reflection of our heart attitude in sowing.

> Matt 6:19-21 19 "Do not store up for yourselves treasures on earth, where moth and rust destroy, and where thieves break in and steal. 20 But store up for yourselves treasures in heaven, where moth and rust do not destroy, and where thieves do nōt break in and steal. 21 For where your treasure is, there your heart will be also."

God knows what we treasure and what we value because it is revealed in our heart. Jesus says where our treasure is, there will our heart be also. If we treasure our paycheck or money then our heart will be with money, possessions, and material things. Our heart will thus desire physical things of the earth and earthly gain will be our satisfaction. Our reward will be in the earth, temporal, where moth and rust can corrupt and where thieves break through and steal.

However, if we treasure God's word then our heart's desire will be to know that Word and be obedient to its instructions. Therefore, our heart would be satisfied with sharing our abundance with the poor and the needy. Our treasure, our reward would be in heaven where neither moth nor rust can corrupt and where thieves do not break through or steal.

> Matthew 6:22-24 "The eye is the lamp of the body. If your eyes are good, your whole body will be full of light. 23But if your eyes are bad, your whole body will be full of darkness. If then the light within you is darkness, how great is that darkness! 24"No one can serve two masters. Either he will hate the one and love the other, or he will be devoted to the one and despise the other. You cannot serve both God and Money."

Jesus continues with His revelation in Matthew 6 and connects verses 19-21 to verses 22–24. What we treasure is dependent upon what our eye is focused on. Jesus says the eye is the lamp of the body.

Our eye can be fixed on good or heavenly things or our eye can be fixed on evil. When our eye is single focused on good, then the eyes of our heart are flooded with light so that we can know and understand the hope to which God has called us and how rich is His glorious inheritance in the saints. (Ephesians 1:18, 19) Our heart is illuminated with the truth and we are the light of the world. (Matthew 5:14, 16). Our light will shine before men, our good works will be seen by them, we store up treasures in heaven for our selves and we bring glory to God our Father in Heaven.

Our eye cannot be focused on both good and evil at the same time. It's either one or the other. When we allow our eyes to roam between good and evil we are actually producing darkness in our bodies. For when the eyes are fixed on evil of any kind our body is full of darkness. Eventually we'll have to choose what light we are going to follow, either the true light of heaven (good) or the false light of darkness (evil). Light and darkness cannot co-exist in our bodies; they are true opposites. Our bodies will give into one and reject the other. Our bodies can not serve both evil and good; we must choose which one it will follow. In Matthew 6:19-21, Jesus is talking about treasure. Our bodies will have to choose what treasure it is going to pursue; the eternal treasure in heaven or the temporary treasure in the earth. The treasure in earth is money and can only give the things money can buy. The treasure in heaven is God. We can't serve both God and money. We will either love God or hate money or we will love money and hate God. We will either be devoted to God or despise money or we will despise God and be devoted to money. Our actual devotion to God or money does not depend on our intentions or our desire; it begins and ends with what we let inside our eye gate which is the lamp of the body. Are you focusing your eye on good or on evil? Test yourself, judge yourself. Are you letting good rule your body and storing up treasures in heaven, or are you letting evil rule your body and storing up treasures in the earth?

Many people, especially Christians will say they don't love, serve or are not devoted to money. Saying we don't love money is not enough. Showing God we are obedient to His word is the real proof we don't love money. We should consciously make storing up treasure in heaven our focus in life and then let our heart speak for us. Giving to the poor and needy is storing up treasure in heaven. For where our treasure is there too is our heart.

Our Eternal Destiny is tied to the love we have in our heart for the poor and needy

Jesus makes an amazing statement in Matthew 25:31-46: Jesus will judge the works of all the people of the earth, based on whether we provided for the needs of the poor, the sick and the prisoner in the Kingdom of God.

Jesus will Judge all nations:

Matt 25:31-46   "When the Son of Man comes in his glory, and all the angels with him, he will sit on his throne in heavenly glory. 32 All the nations will be gathered before him, and he will separate the people one from another as a shepherd separates the sheep from the goats. 33 He will put the sheep on his right and the goats on his left."

The Righteous will have eternal life:

Matthew 25: 34-40 "Then the King will say to those on his right, 'Come, you who are blessed by my Father; take your inheritance, the kingdom prepared for you since the creation of the world. 35 For I was hungry and you gave me something to eat, I was thirsty and you gave me something to drink, I was a stranger and you invited me in, 36 I needed clothes and you clothed me, I was sick and you looked after me, I was in prison and you came to visit me.' 37 "Then the righteous will answer him, 'Lord, when did we see you hungry and feed you, or thirsty and give you something to drink? 38 When did we see you a stranger and invite you in, or needing clothes and clothe you? 39 When did we see you sick or in prison and go to visit you?'   40 "The King will reply, 'I tell you the truth, whatever you did for one of the least of these brothers of mine, you did for me.'

Others will go away to eternal punishment:

> Matthew 25:41-46   "Then he will say to those on his left, 'Depart from me, you who are cursed, into the eternal fire prepared for the devil and his angels. 42 For I was hungry and you gave me nothing to eat, I was thirsty and you gave me nothing to drink, 43 I was a stranger and you did not invite me in, I needed clothes and you did not clothe me, I was sick and in prison and you did not look after me.' 44 "They also will answer, 'Lord, when did we see you hungry or thirsty or a stranger or needing clothes or sick or in prison, and did not help you?' 45 "He will reply, 'I tell you the truth, whatever you did not do for one of the least of these, you did not do for me.' 46 "Then they will go away to eternal punishment, but the righteous to eternal life."

Our eternal destiny, our eternal reward is based on our showing love for the poor, the hungry, the thirsty, the naked, the homeless, the sick, and the imprisoned. Wow! Jesus will ask us at the judgment of mankind, how did we treat our brethren who are in need? He does not say He will judge us based on whether we came to the Church or the Synagogue every week or how many miracles we performed. Jesus also did not say He would judge us on how many churches did we build or speak at or how successful we are in our career. He will ask: Did we help the poor and needy or did we ignore them? Did we seek our own needs only and neglect the need of the sick, the prisoner, the homeless and those without food or clothing? Jesus didn't see himself separate from the poor, the sick and the imprisoned brethren in the Kingdom. Jesus said whatever we do for the least of these brothers of mine, we have done for Him. Jesus also said, whatever we have not done for the least of these His brothers, we have not done to Him. Caring for Jesus' brothers and sisters is considered righteous. Eternal life is the destiny for those who loved their brothers and sisters in Matthew 25. Those who did not show love by providing for the saints in Christ, their eternal destiny was eternal punishment with Satan and his angels.

1 John 4:20-21 "20 anyone who does not love his brother ... cannot love God ... 21 And he has given us this command: Whoever loves God must also love his brother."

How we show love to the poor and needy saints in Christ directly shows how we love Jesus.

Matthew 25:40 "The King will reply, 'I tell you the truth, whatever you did for one of the least of these brothers of mine, you did for me."

The Spirit of the Lord anointed Jesus to preach the gospel to the poor, to heal and give sight to the blind, to preach deliverance to the prisoners and to free the oppressed. (Luke 4:18). Jesus' work was to help the poor and needy. At one time we all were poor and needy and we needed Christ to free us, heal us, provide for us, deliver us, preach to us and open our eyes. It is with thanksgiving for God's blessings of love and help toward us that we too do the same work Jesus did on this earth to help and love others while we remain on this earth. God has sent us His gift of the Holy Spirit so that we can do the work that Jesus did on this earth and even greater.

John 14:12-13 "12 I tell you the truth, anyone who has faith in me will do what I have been doing. He will do even greater things than these, because I am going to the Father. 13 And I will do whatever you ask in my name, so that the Son may bring glory to the Father."

A Deceitful Heart is Dangerous

> Acts 4:32-35 "All the believers were one in heart and mind. No one claimed that any of his possessions was his own, but they shared everything they had. 33 With great power the apostles continued to testify to the resurrection of the Lord Jesus, and much grace was upon them all. 34 There were no needy persons among them. For from time to time those who owned lands or houses sold them, brought the money from the sales 35 and put it at the apostles' feet, and it was distributed to anyone as he had need."

One of the first organized ministries of the church was to collect and distribute supplies to the poor saints in need. Those who had much gave to those who had little. This truly is the will of God so much so that God judged harshly one couple when they lied to the Spirit of our Lord. They told the Apostle's they were giving their full profit from the sell of their property as an offering to the needy collection fund. However this couple decided in their hearts to deceive God and give only part of their earnings but saying it was the full selling price of the land sold. They assumed the secret of their hearts would not be revealed to the Apostles. God wants all of us to give cheerfully with a willing heart and not with ulterior motives or out of deceit. They could have said they were only going to give a part of their profit from the sale and God would have been fine with that. But instead they purposed in their heart to lie to the Holy Spirit. By bringing money and laying it at the feet of the apostle's they were proclaiming they believed Christians have all things in common. This couple would have been considering their property to not be their own anymore but it would have been fully transferred to the commonwealth of believers to be used for the poor saints.

> Acts5:1-4   "Now a man named Ananias, together with his wife Sapphira, also sold a piece of property. 2With his wife's full knowledge he kept back part of the money for himself, but brought the rest and put it at the apostles' feet. 3Then Peter said, "Ananias, how is it that Satan has so filled your heart that you have lied to the Holy Spirit and have kept for yourself some of the money you received for the land? 4 Didn't it belong to you before it was sold? And after it was sold, wasn't the money at your disposal? What made you think of doing such a thing? You have not lied to men but to God."

Both the husband and the wife, Ananias and Sapphira had opportunities to repent and tell the truth but they both chose to stick with sowing their deception and as a result they both reaped the repercussion of punishment. Public praise was their heart motivation and pocketing some of their profit was their heart deception. The confusing thing here was they could have pocketed some of the money from the sale of the property without punishment. This was a volunteer offering after all. All they had to do was say what they purposed in their heart to give and give it. Instead they chose to misrepresent the truth of the sale, trying to look like cheerful givers who sow generously on the outside (displaying to men) but they were really among those who sowed sparingly and begrudgingly in their heart. God loves a cheerful giver and wanted to make giving with a willingly and joyful heart the foundation of all almsgiving in the Kingdom of God. We must be careful not to do our acts of righteousness before men to be seen by them.

Matthew 6:1 "Be careful not to do your 'acts of righteousness' before men, to be seen by them. If you do, you will have no reward from your Father in heaven."

The church is the ground and pillar of the truth. God's word of instruction given the apostle's for the collection for the poor judged the thoughts and attitude of this couples heart. (See Acts 5:1-11) God made an enormous statement about the power of a purposeful heart in sowing and reaping. A heart purposed to sow according to the good instructions of the LORD will reap good rewards from the LORD; a heart purposed to sow according to our own wicked heart will reap the rewards of a wicked heart.

Jeremiah 17:9-10 "The heart is deceitful above all things and beyond cure. Who can understand it? "I the LORD search the heart and examine the mind, to reward a man according to his conduct, according to what his deeds deserve."

God's standard for giving was established among the early church believers. He gave instructions on how organized collections should be handled for both the giver and the administrator of this service who is responsible for distributing the collected funds for the poor. God gave each believer the tools needed to operate in sincere faith in their giving. Where the will of God is known and followed, faith is displayed in the joyous heart of givers.

I remember the first time I gave with a joyous heart. I was at a convention in Baltimore where Bishop T.D. Jakes was the speaker for the night. God spoke to my heart to give $100.00. First I was shocked, a $100.00 I said! I was comfortable giving $10 to $25 outside

Sunday Church services in the past. I could first feel my heart trying to hold on to the $100 and reason with God to reduce that amount to around say $50.00. That was a good compromise I thought. But God didn't compromise with me. We say we want God to tell us what to give but when He does we not prepared to obey. Our flesh tries to become the authority over God's word. This is normal so don't be alarmed; we just need to let the willing Spirit overcome the weakness of our flesh. The truth is I was working as an Engineer making at least $75,000 a year in the mid 1990's and I could afford easily the offering God asked me to give but I wasn't used to giving offerings of that size. God had to train me to hear Him and obey His word beyond my own comfort level and beyond my own erected strongholds of giving. I erected the $25 maximum offerings not God. I thought I was doing well; I climbed from $1 offerings to $5 to $10 all the way up to $25. Now God jumped me to $100. I could afford it, I had it to give, and I just didn't give it. I gave sparingly and I didn't even know it. Out of ignorance I was a stingy giver and God had to show me I was called to be a generous giver. The joy of the Lord filled my heart that day. When TD Jakes was collecting offerings, he said, I want all my $100 givers to come up here to the stage. Wow, I was a $100 giver and I ran down the aisle from the back of the Civic Center waving my $100 in my hand. This was the beginning of a love affair of giving between God and me. He loves a cheerful giver and I became a generous giver who loves to give to God. My giving has exploded since and every time God has proven Himself to meet our needs.

The joy of the Lord gives us strength to generously give with a purposeful heart which achieves in us works of service that pleases God.

Proverbs 22:9

A generous man will himself be blessed,

for he shares his food with the poor.

The Grace of God Enables Us to Give Generously

Grace the power of God to complete in us what He begins.

Ephesians 2:10 "For we are God's workmanship, created in Christ Jesus to do good works, which God prepared in advance for us to do."

We were created in Christ Jesus to do good works. The good work of giving to the poor and needy is enabled by the grace of God. By His grace we are given everything we need to succeed in doing the works God prepared in advance for us to do.

2 Corinthians 9:8 "And God is able to make all grace abound to you, so that in all things at all times, having all that you need, you will abound in every good work."

Let's take a moment to define some of the words and phrases in 2 Corinthians 9:8 to help reveal the deeper meaning God is conveying to us.

God is able

• Able — the word means capable, powerful, mighty, or strong. Therefore God is mighty. God is powerful. God is Strong. God is capable by His mighty power to make all grace abound toward us! In God's hands is the strength and power we need to do what we are called to do. In God's hands is the power to exalt us to our rightful place in the Kingdom of God.

1 Chronicles 29:12 "Wealth and honor come from you; you are the ruler of all things. In your hands are strength and power to exalt and give strength to all."

God is able to make all grace,

• Grace --- Every favor, mercy and spiritual and earthy blessing which is shown forth. We are living in the dispensation of grace. God's glorious grace which He has freely given to us in the One He loves. God has blessed His children in the heavenly realms with every spiritual blessing in Christ. (Ephesians 1:3) God is able to make favor, mercy, and spiritual and earthly blessings come toward us. God's grace influences our hearts moving us to operate according to His will and ways. His grace is shown forth in us and reflected outwardly so people can see the glorious blessing of God in our lives. Grace is our teacher; it teaches us to say no to ungodliness and worldly passions. Grace teaches us to say yes to live a self-controlled, upright and godly life.

> Titus 2:11-15 "11 For the grace of God that brings salvation has appeared to all men. 12 It teaches us to say "No" to ungodliness and worldly passions, and to live self-controlled, upright and godly lives in this present age, 13 while we wait for the blessed hope-the glorious appearing of our great God and Savior, Jesus Christ, 14 who gave himself for us to redeem us from all wickedness and to purify for himself a people that are his very own, eager to do what is good. 15 These, then, are the things you should teach. Encourage and rebuke with all authority."

God is able to make all grace abound

• Abound — super abound (in quantity and quality), to be in excess, to cause to excel, to have more, to be the better, enough and more to spare, exceed, increase, over and above. To abound is to have more than enough with much left over to spare. It also means to excel, be the better, exceed or increase. You don't have to worry about not having enough; there is plenty to go around and much more where that came from. To abound in God's grace means there would be no lack of favor, no lack of mercy and no lack of spiritual or earthly blessings. All the favor, mercy and blessings of God we need to complete the work are yours. God is mighty and powerful to make all favor, all mercy and all blessings increase over and above in us causing us to excel in the good works of the Lord. God intends for His children to live productive lives whereas they have enough resources to carry out the work He has carved out for us to do. Therein is the reason for His abounding grace to all who believe.

Titus 3:14 "14 Our people must learn to devote themselves to doing what is good, in order that they may provide for daily necessities and not live unproductive lives."

God uses the word all, always and every five times in 2 Corinthians 9:8. These words represent the whole, being thorough, and containing as many as whosoever and whatsoever. God deliberately uses the words ALL, ALWAYS and EVERY to show His ability to provide for us completely, wholly and thoroughly. God makes all grace increase to ensure our need is fully taken care of. Grace will continue to supply what's needed until the job gets done. That means everything we need such as people resources, money, buildings, jobs, materials, equipment, attire, revelation and insight, spiritual guidance and counsel is being supplied to complete God's work.

My God, can you see it's like a punching ball with the elastic rubber band attached to it. You give it a punch with your hand and it moves away from you but it eventually comes back toward you. Punching the ball is like our hand going out to give a righteous offering and the return of the punching ball back to our hand is like God making His all sufficient grace come toward us. It is two actions that look like one action to the necked eye. Punching the ball automatically brings the ball back to us. Just like generously sowing a righteous seed with a cheerful heart will automatically bring back toward us God's reigning grace providing all that's needed to achieve God's work on earth bringing glory to God. All we have to do is be willing to do the work assigned to us by God.

1 Peter 4:10 Each one should use whatever gift he has received to serve others, faithfully administering God's grace in its various forms.

God's grace is sufficient!

And God is able to make all grace abound toward you; that ye, always having all sufficiency in all things;

• Sufficiency — possessing enough to require no aid or support and furnished in abundance for every good work and charitable donation. We will never need any thing else from anyone else to complete the task, the assignment, the service or the charitable deed God gives us to do. God's abundance is sufficient. Out of His glorious riches in Christ Jesus He provides for our every need in our present and our future. Nothing or no one can stop us from achieving God's good purpose predestined in us to will and to do His mighty works on the earth. God is declaring to His Children, My grace is sufficient! He has already made the way out of no way and He won't let anyone or anything get in the way. His sufficient grace starts what needs to be started, stops what needs to be stopped and continues what needs to be continued. Sufficient grace has one focus and that is accomplishing the good work or charitable deed period. God confirms His sufficient grace by enabling us to do the works that Christ did on the earth and even greater works because He goes to the Father. (John 14:12)

Acts 14:3 "So Paul and Barnabas spent considerable time there, speaking boldly for the Lord, who confirmed the message of his grace by enabling them to do miraculous signs and wonders. "

Now let's combine the meanings of the individual words to understand 2 Corinthians 9:8 in a deeper way. Here's the scripture we started with:

> "And God is able to make all grace abound to you, so that in all things at all times, having all that you need, you will abound in every good work." (2 Corinthians 9:8)

2 Corinthians 9:8 Restated:

> And God is capable by His mighty power to make all favor, all mercy and all blessings increase over and above to you causing you to excel and having excess; that you will always possess enough to require no aid or support and furnished in all things to the abounding of every good work and charitable donation.

Wow!!!! "What shall we then say to these things? If god be for us, who can be against us? He that spared not his own Son, but delivered him up for us all, how shall he not with him also freely give us all things?" (Romans 8:32)

Jesus came that we might live an abundant life. A life that is rich! A life that is rich in God's glory; rich in Christ Jesus. Let us receive from God what He freely gave us in Christ, that is, all things! God's grace truly is all sufficient. Thank God for His indescribable gift of grace that empowers us to excel at the good cause of giving towards the need of God's people!

John 10:10b, "I am come that you may have life, and that you may have it more abundantly."

Grace Reigns in the life of the believer through Righteousness

Romans 5:21 " so that, just as sin reigned in death, so also grace might reign through righteousness to bring eternal life through Jesus Christ our Lord.

Christ is the righteousness of God. (1 Corinthians 1:30) Grace comes to us because of Christ obedience; the only sinless one (2 Corinthians 5:21) Christ righteousness totally clothes us, covering our sin with His "sinlessness" and producing in us who believe an image of a sinless man. We are no longer sinners sentenced to eternal death but we are the righteous gifted with eternal life. We cannot earn righteousness; it's a gift of God. Once given the gift of righteousness in Christ Jesus, Grace is available to reign in our lives. We can bear the fruit of righteousness by letting grace reign (i.e. having authority in our lives) through righteousness.

Psalms 112:9 "He has distributed freely [he has given to the poor and needy]; his righteousness (uprightness and right standing with God) endures forever; his horn shall be exalted in honor." AMP

2 Corinthians 9:9 As it is written: "He has scattered abroad his gifts to the poor; his righteousness endures forever."

The child of God who gives to the poor freely and generously your righteousness will endure forever and you will be exalted in honor according to Psalms 112:9 and 2 Corinthians 9:9. The righteousness referred to here is the fruit of righteousness produced as a result of imitating Christ character and actions in giving to the poor. God inspired Paul to use a scripture from the Law in the Old Testament which is our school master (our teaching and instruction manual); a witness of the truth to show us God equates giving generously to the poor as righteous in His sight. This righteous act of letting our money leave our hands and dispersing it to the poor is an act that will never be forgotten by God. In God's Kingdom our righteousness will always be remembered forever. God never forgets the good work that is done especially the outreach to His people.

Hebrews 6:10 "God is not unjust; he will not forget your work and the love you have shown him as you have helped his people and continue to help them."

With diligence in doing good and being kind to God's people the promised reward or blessing is certainly ours to have. God will certainly bless us! (Hebrews 6:11-14) Honor shall be found in our houses. Our acts of righteousness are eternal; it remains forever written on the mind of God. God rewards those who seek His kingdom and His righteousness. He rewards us with the things we need.

Matthew 6:33 "But seek first his kingdom and his righteousness, and all these things will be given to you as well."

If for no other reason we help the weak, poor and needy, be convinced we help ourselves. When we give, by the reward and blessing structure of God, it will be given back to us also.

Luke 6:38 "Give, and it will be given to you. A good measure, pressed down, shaken together and running over, will be poured into your lap. For with the measure you use, it will be measured to you."

When we meet the needs of God's people, God will meet our needs. It's as simple as that!

Proverbs 28:27 "If you give to the poor, your needs will be supplied!" (TLB)

Having mercy on the weak by our act of kindness is sowing into their lives when they really need it. And in return when we really need help in times of trouble and times of sickness God will be there to help us. He will protect us, preserve us and bless us where we are. He will overcome for us the will and desires of our enemies; their plans will not prosper but fail. When we sow on behalf of the weak we reap healing in our mind and body; we are sustained on our sickbed and restored from our bed of illness. We are sowing into the life of the weak to transform them from weakness to strength. We will reap the same when we are weak; God promises to raise us up from a position of weakness to a position of strength. We are blessed because we purposed in our heart to provide for the poor, needy and weak.

> Ps 41:1-3 " 1 Blessed is he who has regard for the weak; the LORD delivers him in times of trouble. 2 The LORD will protect him and preserve his life; he will bless him in the land and not surrender him to the desire of his foes. 3 The LORD will sustain him on his sickbed and restore him from his bed of illness.

Tabitha in Acts 9:36-41 is an example of a person who had regard for the weak. She was well known for doing good works and helping the poor. When she became weak with sickness and died the LORD delivered her. She was blessed by God in her time of trouble. Illness thought it took her life but God's promise to preserve her life overcame her illness that lead to death and restored her from her death bed. Tabitha's life of giving inspired the saints to pray for her and God listened attentively; the power of God was sent to raise Tabitha up from death to life.

Acts 9:36-42 "36 In Joppa there was a disciple named Tabitha (which, when translated, is Dorcas), who was always doing good and helping the poor. 37 About that time she became sick and died, and her body was washed and placed in an upstairs room. 38 Lydda was near Joppa; so when the disciples heard that Peter was in Lydda, they sent two men to him and urged him, "Please come at once!" 39 Peter went with them, and when he arrived he was taken upstairs to the room. All the widows stood around him, crying and showing him the robes and other clothing that Dorcas had made while she was still with them. 40 Peter sent them all out of the room; then he got down on his knees and prayed. Turning toward the dead woman, he said, "Tabitha, get up." She opened her eyes, and seeing Peter she sat up. 41 He took her by the hand and helped her to her feet. Then he called the believers and the widows and presented her to them alive."

Yes, it's true! A generous man will prosper. He who refreshes others will himself be refreshed! (Proverbs 11:25)   Do You Believe?

Righteousness is the Key to Prosperity!

God has something to say about that...

Proverbs 13:21 "Misfortune pursues the sinner, but prosperity is the reward of the righteous."

Proverbs 11:18 ".but he who sows righteousness reaps a sure reward."

Proverbs 21:21 "He who pursues righteousness and love finds life, prosperity and honor."

Hosea 10:12 "Sow for yourselves righteousness, reap the fruit of unfailing love …"

Everyone who serves God in righteousness is pleasing to God and approved by men. The Kingdom of God is righteousness in the Holy Spirit. (Romans 14:17-18)

Eph 5:8-10 8 "For you were once darkness, but now you are light in the Lord. Live as children of light 9(for the fruit of the light consists in all goodness, righteousness and truth) 10 and find out what pleases the Lord."

Warning: Be careful not to do your "acts of righteousness" before men to be seen by them. If we do we will have no reward from God. So when we give to the needy do not announce it on a bull horn, to the news paper or yell it in the streets for all to hear to be honored by men. When our hearts motivation to give is to be acknowledged by people, God says we already have our reward from men; there is no need for God to reward us also. If we want God's reward for giving to the needy, we should do our giving in secret. God describes giving in secret as not even letting our left hand know what our right hand is doing. Now that is truly secret. Simply put, we should not toot our own horn and we should keep silent about our giving. We should not seek to exalt our selves but we should trust God to do so. When God sees what is done in secret, He is faithful to reward us.

> Matthew 6:1-4 6:1 "Be careful not to do your 'acts of righteousness' before men, to be seen by them. If you do, you will have no reward from your Father in heaven. 2 "So when you give to the needy, do not announce it with trumpets, as the hypocrites do in the synagogues and on the streets, to be honored by men. I tell you the truth, they have received their reward in full. 3 But when you give to the needy, do not let your left hand know what your right hand is doing, 4 so that your giving may be in secret. Then your Father, who sees what is done in secret, will reward you."

The Lord God Himself rewards each of us according to the deeds we have done. God examines our heart and mind to determine what rewards we deserve.

> Jeremiah 17:10 "I the LORD search the heart and examine the mind, to reward a man according to his conduct, according to what his deeds deserve."

God doesn't ask us what reward we deserve, nor does He ask our pastor, family, friends or enemies what reward we should get for the deeds we have done on the earth. God goes right to the places of memory in our bodies, the heart and the mind, which displays our whole life to God from start to finish truthfully. God judges our heart and mind according to His righteous standards. Our acts of righteousness will pass the judgment of God and will gain us well deserved rewards from God who graciously gives them to us.

In Isaiah 58:7-8, God's word says when you share your food with the hungry and provide the poor wanderer with shelter—when you see the naked and clothe him, and do not turn away from your own flesh and blood then your light will break forth like the dawn, and your healing will quickly appear. God goes on and says our righteousness will go before us, and the glory of the LORD will be our rear guard.

The righteous acts of feeding the hungry, providing shelter and clothes for the poor and oppressed and taking care of your own flesh and blood, causes our righteousness to go before us and the glory of the Lord to move on our behalf behind us. God goes before us because of our giving and He guards our backside because of our righteousness. You are protected and cared for by God because we followed God's instruction to give or sow into the lives of those who lacked financially, materially and/or spiritually.

Cornelius righteous acts of giving to the poor and prayer came up to God as a memorial offering. He consistently gave gifts to the poor and regularly prayed at daily times of prayer as did the Jews. Cornelius was a Gentile whom the Jewish people respected and they called him righteous and God fearing. He and his family were devout believers in the one God, the God of the Jews. And God rewarded his regular prayer and giving to the poor by making Cornelius and His family one of the first Gentiles to receive Salvation in Jesus Christ as Lord and Savior. (Acts 10:30-48)

Acts 10:1-4 "1 At Caesarea there was a man named Cornelius, a centurion in what was known as the Italian Regiment. 2 He and all his family were devout and God-fearing; he gave generously to those in need and prayed to God regularly. 3 One day at about three in the afternoon he had a vision. He distinctly saw an angel of God, who came to him and said, "Cornelius!" 4 Cornelius stared at him in fear. "What is it, Lord?" he asked. The angel answered, "Your prayers and gifts to the poor have come up as a memorial offering before God."

God remembered forever Cornelius gifts to the poor and his righteousness went before him. As a result, heaven caused or made grace increase for Cornelius and his family. An angel ministered to him God's instruction that would lead him to his future destiny. Cornelius righteous acts moved the heart and hand of God on his behalf. God sent Peter the Jewish Apostle to teach the word of God to this Gentile family that would make Cornelius and his family part of God's family forever. God prepared a harvest of righteousness for Cornelius to reap. The harvest prepared for him and his family was to be among the first Gentiles to receive God's covenant of Salvation in Jesus Christ. God just didn't prepare the harvest for Cornelius, but he ensured Cornelius and his family would receive the fullness of the harvest by providing the weight of His glory, splendor and honor as Cornelius' rear guard. God's word always accomplishes what it was sent out to do. God enlarged the fruit of Cornelius' righteousness enabling him to partake of God's glorious riches in Christ Jesus so that he could be richer and more generous on every occasion.

My Prayer for all believers is that we are filled with the fruit of righteousness that comes through Christ Jesus because of our acts of righteousness in giving to the poor. Our righteousness will surely go before us and the glory of God will be our rear guard accomplishing in us God's magnificent plan for our lives.

> Phil 1:9-11 "9 And this is my prayer: that your love may abound more and more in knowledge and depth of insight, 10 so that you may be able to discern what is best and may be pure and blameless until the day of Christ, 11 filled with the fruit of righteousness that comes through Jesus Christ-to the glory and praise of God."

3 John 3-8

3 In fact, I greatly rejoiced when [some of] the brethren from time to time arrived and spoke [so highly] of the sincerity and fidelity of your life, as indeed you do live in the Truth [the whole Gospel presents]. 4 I have no greater joy than this, to hear that my [spiritual] children are living their lives in the Truth. 5 Beloved, it is a fine and faithful work that you are doing when you give any service to the [Christian] brethren, and [especially when they are] strangers. 6 They have testified before the church of your love and friendship. You will do well to forward them on their journey [and you will please do so] in a way worthy of God's [service]. 7 For these [traveling missionaries] have gone out for the Name's sake (for His sake) and are accepting nothing from the Gentiles (the heathen, the non-Israelites). 8 So we ourselves ought to support such people [to welcome and provide for them], in order that we may be fellow workers in the Truth (the whole Gospel) and cooperate with its teachers.

AMP

Sow the Seed in Your Hand and Reap a Multiplied Harvest

Sharing in the Matter of Giving and Receiving

2 Corinthians 9:10-11 "10 Now he who supplies seed to the sower and bread for food will also supply and increase your store of seed and will enlarge the harvest of your righteousness. 11 You will be made rich in every way so that you can be generous on every occasion."

When we are "sowers" of God's seed, He has the pleasure of increasing our wealth by two means:

1. Supplying and Increasing the store of our seed and

2. Enlarging the harvest of our righteousness

The purpose of sowing the seed God has placed in our hands is so we will reap a harvest of bread to eat and more seed to sow again. The righteous "sower" is made rich in every way so that they can be generous at all times. God's standard for giving is Generosity. He rose up this standard to heal poverty in the Kingdom by the love we show for one another and to show forth His glory to the world. Once we catch a hold of the spirit of generous giving we won't want to let it go. God makes us rich for one purpose: To give us what we need to make us even more generous. God has planned it so the righteous giver can have overflow at all times so we can be generous on every occasion when someone is in need. God truly gave us Jesus Christ so we as a body will not lack any good thing. Will you arise with me to this truth, believing God, testing Him and proving Him Faithful?

The Double Blessing

Blessed with seed in one hand to sow and blessed with bread in the other hand to eat!

- God supplies us with bread to eat

We won't have to worry about our family, if they will have food to eat or if our basic needs will be met. (Psalms 37:25 "I was young and now I am old, yet I have never seen the righteous forsaken or their children begging bread.")

- God supplies us with the seed to sow

The income we receive on earth has a seed contained in it so we can sow. All we have to do is plant it in the lives of God's people and be careful not to eat the seed God provides for us.

(Proverbs 3:9-10 " 9 Honor the LORD with your wealth, with the firstfruits of all your crops; 10 then your barns will be filled to overflowing, and your vats will brim over with new wine.")

- God multiplies the seed we sow

We plant the seed into righteous ground (God's people) and God is faithful to multiply our seed sown. We are not responsible for the increase in our seed, God is and He will prove His Word. Man knows not how a seed grows, but man recognizes the harvest when it comes and it is man whom God ordains to reap it. (Mark 4:26-29). God increases our seed to allow us to give more the next time. As we are faithful to sow the seed God gives us, God increases our seed so that we can be generous in every way, every time an opportunity to give presents itself. It is God who ensures we are provided with seed to give. God is the provider for all the needs of His people. Each child of God is a funnel through which God can provide for the needs of His children.

(2 Chronicles 31:10 ....."Since the people began to bring their contributions to the temple of the LORD, we have had enough to eat and plenty to spare, because the LORD has blessed his people, and this great amount is left over.")

- God increases the harvest of our righteousness

Our righteous acts of giving to the poor and needy are recognized by God as good works and as a results God empowers us to do even more good works. Thereby increasing the harvest or fruit of our righteousness. We must be united to Jesus Christ in order to bring forth a harvest of righteousness. It is God who causes us to bear fruit. It is God who has chosen us to bring forth a harvest; a harvest as a result of doing what is righteous in the sight of God. He has appointed us, as followers of Christ, to bear fruit that is everlasting to God's glory. God increases the fruit of our righteousness as we submit to His word and follow Him in giving. In this way we prove ourselves to be Disciples of Christ Jesus our LORD. (John 15:8 "This is to my Father's glory, that you bear much fruit, showing yourselves to be my disciples.")

God is our only source for bread to eat and seed to sow.

Isaiah 55:10 "As the rain and the snow come down from heaven, and do not return to it without watering the earth and making it bud and flourish, so that it yields seed for the sower and bread for the eater,"

God is the giver of everything we have and shall have in the future. Everything we have in our pockets, anything we have invested, everything we have stored in the bank, every material possession, and everything we have accumulated comes from God. This must be a foundational understanding that guides our actions.

Everything that God makes has a natural seed within it. Every fruit, vegetable, tree, plant, animal and every human has seed in it to reproduce after its own kind, enabling the seed to produce a harvest.

A harvest is made up of two parts: the consumable part of the harvest such as food we eat or clothing we wear and the part of the harvest that contains more seed to sow. We must be able to tell the difference between a seed given from the harvest to sow and increase and the part of the harvest given to consume. For example, a potato farmer's crop contains a harvest to be eaten by family, friends and anyone the farmer shares with or sells to. The farmer recognizes that the potato harvest he reaped contains potato seed that can be sown to produce another eatable harvest next potato growing season. A farmer learns to separate out the consumable harvest from the seed within the harvest. He will use the consumable harvest for its intended use, food and sow the seed harvest for its intended use to grow a new potato crop. If the farmer does not sow part of His potato crop back into the ground there won't be a new potato crop the next year because He ate His seed putting an end to seed multiplication. If the seed is not sown it can not be multiplied; it is only good for today and it has no future benefit. What a waste!

Many people today are not farmers but many go to work and receive a paycheck. We must be able to see the paycheck as both containing a seed to sow and a harvest to consume. Now the trick is to determine what part of the paycheck is a seed to be sown and which part is the harvest to be consumed for our family obligations such as paying bills, eating, etc. In every income increase, such as earnings from the sale of stock, gift from grandma, bonus at work, etc. there are always going to be both seed and bread. I know I am putting a lot of emphasis on this point. I didn't want anyone reading this book to float off to "reasoning land", excusing any of their income increase from containing seed. Seed belongs to God and is required to be sown and not consumed.

My People Reason too Much!

I am empathetic to the possibility that many reading this book might be in so much debt at this time that they can't even take care of their family obligations with the income they have. They either don't make enough money or they have overspent in the past and now do not have enough to take care of all the expenses.

The question is how can we sow according to God's word and pay our bills when we don't have enough income for both?

The answer is by God's grace.

The follow up question usually is: doesn't God want me to pay my bills?

The answer is yes.

Then we say, how can we do both?

Excessive reasoning sets in at this point. This is the place where many people turn away from God's Word. They focus on their current circumstances and their lack instead of on the power of God to deliver them. Reasoning too much puts bill paying in competition with sowing. Here's where people get nervous. Reasoning too much will put you in the survival of the fittest mode; you tend to believe only you can do what's needed to make you and your family survive. Righteousness is the way to survive for believers. Reasoning too much will make us blind to the blessing of obeying God. God tells us not to worry about what we will eat or what clothes we will wear, the Gentiles (those not under the covenant of God) do this. (Matthew 6:25-32) We are the covenant people of God who seek after the Kingdom of God and His righteousness and all these things will be, not might be, but will be added unto us who have faith in Jesus Christ. (Matthew 6:33) This should be our focus. However, the normal response is to ponder such things as:

- If I sow my seed instead of paying my bills my electric will get turned off and how then does my family cook and eat?

- If I don't pay my rent my family won't have a place to live.

- If I choose to sow a seed but can't pay my car note I won't have a car to drive to work and I'll loose my Job. I won't have a seed or a harvest if I loose my job. So I can't see my way to sow a seed until I can get myself out of this financial mess.

The conclusion many come to is God will understand if I don't sow seed at this time; He sees my problem and God knows my heart. The truth is it is our heart that got us in this situation to begin with; … out of the heart flow the issues of life. (Proverbs 4:23) This statement is not meant to offend anyone but to help us. It's also true, God sees our current situations and longs to help us to get out of debt and prosper. I'm not just preaching here, I'm familiar with being in this situation myself and I'm familiar with the reasons my husband and I used to justify why we couldn't sow.

We had two mortgages, house bills, two car notes, credit cards, loans and child care debt. We depended on both incomes to pay for our lifestyle. My husband and I were Christians at this time, we just started to consistently tithe and give offerings and alms when my husband lost His job. The next time I was writing out checks for bills I immediately reasoned we could not afford to give our tithe and offerings anymore until God blessed my husband with another job. In our reality, if we paid our tithes we would not have enough to pay our bills and yes I said it "God you do want me to pay my bills don't you?" I gave no thought to the fact God didn't direct me to run up credit card bills. I gave no thought to decreasing our current lifestyle, but I did give thought quickly to relinquishing God's command of bringing my tithes and offerings into the storehouse of the Lord (Malachi 3:10). I didn't have enough spiritual maturity at this time to know that my faith must stand in the word of God and not in my current situation or circumstance no matter how daunting it seemed to be. My husband and mine reasoning prevailed over our obedience to God's word and we seemed to get more and more into debt. We were behind in many of our bills. Until one day the grace of God got my attention when I was in prayer. God prompted me to ask Him this question: Which do I pay, my bills or your tithe? God's response to me was to turn on the T.V. right then and there, and I obeyed. Immediately when I turned on the T.V., on the channel was a preacher and the very first thing I heard him say, and I'm not exaggerating, "your tithes should be paid first and your bills after."

I was in Awe. My God is faithful. I knew the answer to the question now. It was to pay God's tithe first and I started doing just that out of faith in His word consistently from that day. The fruit of God's word produced bills paid on time instead of late and God prompted my family to get out of debt. This was very hard work. We consciously decreased our spending and we did not use credit or loans for any new purchases. Strengthened by God, five years later we were debt free with the exception of our mortgage. Praise God! When we stopped our excessive reasoning, God was able to get our attention and cause His blessing to be showered upon us. He freed us from buying on credit what we could not pay off in thirty days. He taught us to spend only the money we have and to not spend over that amount. He freed us from the bondage of debt. He taught us that His word in bringing tithes and offerings is superior to our bill paying. We were taught bill paying is also required by God, for God says we are to owe no man except to love him.

Romans 13:8 "Owe no man any thing, but to love one another:"

God's Word always prevails. We stopped robbing God and God really proved to us that when we bring our tithes and offerings He does open the windows of heaven and pours out a blessing that we don't have room enough to contain. (Malachi 3:8-10) We thank God that He is faithful even we are not.

For everyone who has to make the tough choice of deciding who to pay first, your creditors or God? I would suggest that you test and prove God, making Him first, by honoring Him with your tithe and offerings. Then have faith in God; trusting Him to help you pay your other bills. If possible reduce your spending, increase your income and get out of debt.

Sowing the seed God has given us is the way to increase our store of seed and increase the harvest of our righteousness, which manifests itself in active goodness, kindness, and charity in the Kingdom. When seed is eaten there can be no multiplication and it seems as if we can get no where fast no matter how hard we try. It seems that the harder we push forward the deeper in debt we become when we don't sow the seed given us by God. There will always be what seem to be valid reasons for eating our seed, i.e. not tithing or given our offerings, but that's the devourer trying to scare you and trying to deceive you. Sowing our seed stops the devourer from eating our harvest (Malachi 3:11).

Let God be the Lord of the Harvest in your life so that He will cause you to bear good fruit that last. God will by the power of His grace cause us to produce good fruit in ever increasing proportions. Sowing seed becomes the gift that keeps on giving causing us to impact more people's lives with His love. God causes us to bestow more mercy, to be even more generous, to operate even greater in His gifts, and to fulfill His purposes with greater fervency.

God teaches us how to experience the perpetual Seed-Harvest He designed for those who love Him. When we look at it with our spiritual eye we can see what God has created. Every harvest contains bread for food and seed to sow. Every seed sown produces harvest which also contains both bread and seed to sow again. Do you see how God's seed ministered to you has the very real ability to produce for you and the Kingdom of God a perpetual harvest? Perpetual means continuous, having no end. This is God's will for His children. We can experience God's perfect will manifested visibly in our life if we are willing to follow God's plan of seed-harvest (giving-receiving). Let's all make a decision to reserve the seed and sow it consistently.

For all of us who desire to partake of God's totality of provision and submit to His way of handling those provisions we will have all we need and abundantly more. This is the wealth making power of God! He supernaturally multiplies every seed we sow, so we have more and more seed to sow. God also supernaturally increases our harvest for us to enjoy.

The Wealth Making Power of God

Wealth and riches are in the house of the righteous.

Psalms 112:1-3 "1 Blessed is the man who fears the LORD, who finds great delight in his commands. 2 His children will be mighty in the land; the generation of the upright will be blessed. 3 Wealth and riches are in his house, and his righteousness endures forever."

Wealth is bought to those who are humble and fear the LORD.

Proverbs 22:4 "Humility and the fear of the LORD bring wealth and honor and life."

Wealth is stored up for and handed to the man who pleases God.

Ecclesiastes 2:26 "To the man who pleases him, God gives wisdom, knowledge and happiness, but to the sinner he gives the task of gathering and storing up wealth to hand it over to the one who pleases God."

God's Word lights the pathway to receive of His glorious riches, making us rich in Christ. Disciple's being wealthy is not the end of God's point; God commands the rich to not be arrogant or put our hope in wealth but to be rich in good deeds and to be generous and willing to share.

> 1 Timothy 6:17-19 "Command those who are rich in this present world not to be arrogant nor to put their hope in wealth, which is so uncertain, but to put their hope in God, who richly provides us with everything for our enjoyment. 18 Command them to do good, to be rich in good deeds, and to be generous and willing to share. 19 In this way they will lay up treasure for themselves as a firm foundation for the coming age, so that they may take hold of the life that is truly life."

A man who is rich toward God gains even more. A man who is stingy or withholds from God comes to poverty.

Proverbs 11:24 "One man gives freely, yet gains even more; another withholds unduly, but comes to poverty."

A righteous seed sown lays up heavenly treasure for you and brings thanksgiving and glory to God. The wealth of the Kingdom of God is in the hands of Jesus' Disciples.

Revelation 1:5-6

To him who loves us and has freed us from our sins by his blood,

6 and has made us to be a kingdom and priests to serve his God

and Father-to him be glory and power for ever and ever!

Amen.

Submitting to the Gospel of Jesus Christ in Our Giving

In Service to God

The Service we perform brings praise and thanksgiving to God.

> 2 Corinthians 9:12-13   "12 This service that you perform is not only supplying the needs of God's people but is also overflowing in many expressions of thanks to God. 13 Because of the service by which you have proved yourselves, men will praise God for the obedience that accompanies your confession of the gospel of Christ, and for your generosity in sharing with them and with everyone else."

The church at Achaia promised to perform the Service of God by supplying the needs of God's people. Yes giving to the poor is considered service to God. Service is defined as performing a public function such as an almsgiver, performing religious or charitable functions such as worship also to obey, relieve, aid, minister or administer. The Church at Achaia made a vow to serve as an almsgiver to relieve the poverty of the saints. When they vowed they fully agreed openly with their mouths for all to hear. A vow is a confession or a profession that obligates us to do what we said we would do. The administrators of this service took the church of Achaia at their word and to say nothing of God, would not want to see them break their word.

God has something to say about Vows...

> Deuteronomy 23:21-23   "21 If you make a vow to the LORD your God, do not be slow to pay it, for the LORD your God will certainly demand it of you and you will be guilty of sin. 22 But if you refrain from making a vow, you will not be guilty. 23 Whatever your lips utter you must be sure to do, because you made your vow freely to the LORD your God with your own mouth."

When we make a vow freely with our mouth, God certainly demands us to keep it.

Numbers 30:1, 2   "This is what the LORD commands: 2 When a man makes a vow to the LORD or takes an oath to obligate himself by a pledge, he must not break his word but must do everything he said."

When a man makes a vow to the LORD or takes an oath to obligate him by a pledge, he must not break his word but must do everything he said. A promise or vow broken is a sin. A vow cannot be canceled except for these two ways according to Numbers 30:1-16:

1. A vow made by an unmarried daughter living in her father's household can be canceled by her Father.

2. A vow made by a wife can be canceled by her husband.

A vow made by a man can not be cancelled and must be fulfilled. We are to not hastily make a vow. We are to think carefully first before obligating our self. In the American culture we don't always hold promises as sacred and honorable to be fulfilled. God doesn't excuse us for our culture. Our obedience is not subjected to our natural culture any longer but to our spiritual culture as defined by the King in the Kingdom of God, where we are citizens. If you have made a vow or promise in the past that you haven't kept, don't feel guilty. Do the following: If it's within your control, fulfill the vow. If it is out of your control, go to our Father and ask for forgiveness and He is faithful and just to forgive you and cleanse you of all your unrighteousness by the blood of Jesus Christ. (1 John 1:9) And go and sin no more.

To make a vow is one thing. To prove ourselves faithful to fulfill the vow is another. God gets the praise, honor and glory for the works of service performed by His grace not just the works talked about.

1 John 3:18, 19 "Dear children, let us not love with words or tongue but with actions and in truth. 19 This then is how we know that we belong to the truth,"

If the church of Achaia fulfills their promise to give, men will praise God for the obedience that accompanies their confession of the gospel of Christ and for their generosity in sharing with them. When the church at Achaia professed their faith in the gospel of Christ at their conversion, they fully agreed to follow (be disciples) of Christ, imitating Him. For we know how generous our Lord Jesus the Messiah was – for our sakes He impoverished Himself, even though He was rich, so that He might make us rich by means of His poverty. (2 Corinthians 8:9). The church of Achaia promised to be like Christ, following His lead by also enriching the poor people of God with the riches God has entrusted to them.

The church of Achaia's motivation to give should be based on their submission to the gospel of Jesus Christ. Would they pay attention to the wisdom of God and keep His words in the midst of their hearts? Or would they forsake God's wisdom and opt to follow the world's wisdom? God exhorts us not to conform to this world but to be transformed by the renewing of our mind with His wisdom. The message of the cross (the gospel of Christ) is the power of God for everyone who is saved.

1 Corinthians 1:18   "For the message of the cross is foolishness to those who are perishing, but to us who are being saved it is the power of God."

God promises to destroy worldly wisdom and frustrate worldly intelligence.

1 Corinthians 1:19, 20 "19 For it is written: "I will destroy the wisdom of the wise; the intelligence of the intelligent I will frustrate." 20 Where is the wise man? Where is the scholar? Where is the philosopher of this age? Has not God made foolish the wisdom of the world?"

From the book of Genesis to Revelation, giving is the Lord's will. He takes the foolish things of this world to confound the wise. In God's Kingdom you have to give in order to be rich – this is foolishness to the world. The wisdom of the world says in order to get more you have to take more.

There is no wisdom greater than God's!

1 Corinthians 1:25 "For the foolishness of God is wiser than man's wisdom, and the weakness of God is stronger than man's strength."

Whether you are wise by human standards or not, whether you are born into nobility or have great influence or not it is all foolishness as compared with the wisdom of God. God's ways are higher than our ways. He chooses what the world considers foolish or lowly and exalts it to shame the wise, noble and influential in the world. God's children live in this world but we are not of this world therefore we are not to operate in the wisdom of this world. We are to operate in the greater wisdom; the wisdom of God through Christ Jesus.

> 1 Corinthians 1:26-31   "26 Brothers, think of what you were when you were called. Not many of you were wise by human standards; not many were influential; not many were of noble birth. 27 But God chose the foolish things of the world to shame the wise; God chose the weak things of the world to shame the strong. 28 He chose the lowly things of this world and the despised things-and the things that are not-to nullify the things that are, 29 so that no one may boast before him. 30 It is because of him that you are in Christ Jesus, who has become for us wisdom from God-that is, our righteousness, holiness and redemption.   31 Therefore, as it is written: "Let him who boasts boast in the Lord.""

Therefore let him who boasts, boast in the Lord. Let Him who boast, boast in the wisdom of God. Giving to the needy people of God is wise and gives everyone a reason to boast in the LORD, both the needy who is the receiver of the blessing and the generous giver who is blessed to be a blessing. Exercising kindness, justice and righteousness is what delights God! Delight the Lord with your giving. Those who delight in the Lord, He will give them the desires of their heart. (Psalms 37:4)

> Jeremiah 9:23-24 "23 This is what the LORD says: "Let not the wise man boast of his wisdom or the strong man boast of his strength or the rich man boast of his riches, 24 but let him

who boasts boast about this: that he understands and knows me, that I am the LORD, who exercises kindness, justice and righteousness on earth, for in these I delight," declares the LORD."

It is important that the Administrators of the gifts for the needy understands and knows the LORD and what delights Him. What delights God is that we are kind to one another, and when we see injustice we fight for justice extending the righteousness of God on the earth. James, Peter and John understood what delighted the LORD and they made sure Paul knew also. In Galatians 2:9, 10, the Apostles blessed Paul in the work God had called him to do and agreed he should go to the Gentiles to witness Christ Jesus. They only asked Paul to do one thing, to remember the poor. Paul was very enthusiastic to do this very thing.

> Galatians 2:9, 10 "9 James, Peter and John, those reputed to be pillars, gave me and Barnabas the right hand of fellowship when they recognized the grace given to me. They agreed that we should go to the Gentiles, and they to the Jews. 10All they asked was that we should continue to remember the poor, the very thing I was eager to do."

Paul agreed and was eager to perform this service of God that delighted Him by ensuring the needs of the poor were addressed. Paul was instructed to bring Alms to the Nation of Jerusalem and he obeyed.

The Bible records Paul's obedience to this service of God in the following scriptures:

Acts 24:17 "After an absence of several years, I came to Jerusalem to bring my people gifts for the poor and to present offerings."

Acts 11:29-30 "29 The disciples, each according to his ability, decided to provide help for the brothers living in Judea. 30 This they did, sending their gift to the elders by Barnabas and Saul."

> 1 Corinthians 16:1-4 "1 Now about the collection for God's people: Do what I told the Galatian churches to do. 2 On the first day of every week, each one of you should set aside a sum

of money in keeping with his income, saving it up, so that when I come no collections will have to be made. 3 Then, when I arrive, I will give letters of introduction to the men you approve and send them with your gift to Jerusalem. 4 If it seems advisable for me to go also, they will accompany me."

Bringing the Gift of Alms to the Nation of Jerusalem

Jerusalem is the capital of Israel and its largest city. It's the place of blessing. Jerusalem is:

- The Holy City of God (Isaiah 52:1, Rev 21:10)

- The City of the Great King (Matthew 5:35)

- City of Truth (Zechariah 8:3)

- The place of Christ's Death, Burial, Resurrection and Ascension (Luke 18:31-32)

- The birthplace of the Church (Acts 2)

- The place of outpouring of the Holy Spirit upon all flesh at Pentecost (Acts 2:1-4)

- Witnessing of the gospel of Jesus Christ (repentance and forgiveness of sin) started in Jerusalem (Luke 24:47)

It is the poor saints in Jerusalem that God wanted blessed in 2 Corinthians chapter 9. The promised donation of generous alms would go to bless those in God's Holy City.

Paul wasn't performing this service alone, Titus and the other chosen teachers and administrators needed to have the same spiritual understanding to accomplish the goal of blessing God's people with alms. All the administrators had to prove they were honest and trustworthy to collect the funds for the poor, deliver the funds and distribute the funds as they promised. They would want to avoid any criticism of the way they administered the generous gift, taking pains to do what's right in the eyes of the Lord and in the eyes of men. (2 Corinthians 8:19-23)

Every one chosen to be responsible for the finances in the Kingdom of God must represent the church respectfully and honor Christ by the works of their hand in the strength God provides.

> 1 Peter 4:10-11 "10 Each one should use whatever gift he has received to serve others, faithfully administering God's grace in its various forms. 11 If anyone serves, he should do it with the strength God provides, so that in all things God may be praised through Jesus Christ. To him be the glory and the power for ever and ever. Amen."

Paul credits Jesus Christ with giving him the strength to perform the service of the saints which our Lord appointed him to. He declares it was the grace of our Lord that was abundantly poured out on him to complete every work of service. (1 Timothy 1:12, 14) By serving in the strength God provides we are letting our light shine before man that they will see our good deeds bringing praise and glory to God. (Matthew 5:16)

What does in the strength of God mean? It is another way of saying it's by the grace of God.

Doing our works of service in the grace of God acknowledges that God is the provider of all things even our strength to accomplish everything we do, our strength to be everything we are and our strength to share everything we have. David couldn't have put it better than in

1 Chronicles 29:11-16:

11 Yours, O LORD, is the greatness and the power

and the glory and the majesty and the splendor,

for everything in heaven and earth is yours.

Yours, O LORD, is the kingdom;

you are exalted as head over all.

12 Wealth and honor come from you;

you are the ruler of all things.

In your hands are strength and power

to exalt and give strength to all.

13 Now, our God, we give you thanks,

and praise your glorious name.

14 "But who am I, and who are my people,

that we should be able to give as generously

as this? Everything comes from you, and we

have given you only what comes from your hand.

15 We are aliens and strangers in your sight, as

were all our forefathers. Our days on earth are

like a shadow, without hope. 16 O LORD our God,

as for all this abundance that we have provided

for building you a temple for your Holy Name,

it comes from your hand, and all of it belongs to you

Everything in heaven and on earth is the LORD's; greatness, power, splendor and majesty is His. He is exalted as head over all and ruler over all. His is the Kingdom. Wealth, honor and glory come from the LORD. It is in God's hands alone to give strength to all. Without God's strength we have no strength that would last. Everything we have comes from God and when we give, we are given what God first gave to us. It is God who gives us hope and provides us abundantly. It all comes from His hand and it all belongs to Him. Now, Oh LORD, we give you thanks and praise your glorious name.

God's Surpassing Grace

2 Corinthians 9:14-15 "14 And in their prayers for you their hearts will go out to you, because of the surpassing grace God has given you. 15 Thanks be to God for his indescribable gift!"

God's surpassing grace enables us to do what God has ordained for us to do. Every service, every different kinds of working, every gift, and every ministry performed by men, is worked out in us by God. (1 Corinthians 12:4-6)

By depending on the grace of God, we rightly perform our works of service on the foundation of Jesus Christ. There are other foundations in this world by which we can build on that will not last such as money, materials, possessions, education, our family name, business or career. At the proper time all of our work will be shown for what it is in the light of Jesus Christ. The quality of all our work will be tested and proven by fire. If what we have built survives the testing then we will receive our reward. For God is a consuming fire. (Hebrews 12:29). If our work is burned up, it is judged we built it on a foundation other than Jesus Christ. All will be lost and no reward will be given. Believers, whose work is built on any other foundation than Jesus Christ, will be saved but their work will be burned up. Believers can be saved having an eternal home in heaven as one escaping through the flames but on earth their works of serving, leadership, teaching and even giving are enabled by worldly or human wisdom, power and strength void of God's grace. In the Day of Judgment, everyman's work will testify of itself.

1 Corinthians 3:10-15 "10 By the grace God has given me, I laid a foundation as an expert builder, and someone else is building on it. But each one should be careful how he builds. 11 For no one can lay any foundation other than the one already laid, which is Jesus Christ. 12 If any man builds on this foundation using gold, silver, costly stones, wood, hay or straw, 13 his work will be shown for what it is, because the Day will bring it to light. It will be revealed with fire, and the fire will test the quality of each man's work. 14 If what he has built survives, he will receive his reward. 15 If it is burned up, he will

suffer loss; he himself will be saved, but only as one escaping through the flames."

We are to be good stewards of ministering to one another the manifold grace of God. So that in all things God may be praised through Jesus Christ, to who be glory and power forever and ever. Amen. (1 Peter 4:10-11) When God's grace reaches people it always causes thanksgiving to overflow to the glory of God. (2 Corinthians 4:15)

Did the Church at Achaia allow God's grace to reach the poor saints in Jerusalem through their works of service?

Did Paul's letter and Titus' visit encourage them to give what they promised and learn to excel in the Grace of Giving?

Did they pass the Test? You bet they did!

They submitted to the grace of God and the result was an excellent gift that took away the lack of God's people in the Holy City of God, Jerusalem. Paul and the other administrators of the gift were pleased with the contribution and they delivered the gift to Jerusalem. The Jews shared their spiritual jewels with the Gentiles and in return the Gentiles shared their material jewels with them. Everyone in the Kingdom of God had what they needed, no one had too much and no one had too little. Paul was able to fulfill his promise to remember the poor saints in Jerusalem with the help of the faithful in Corinth and in Macedonia to the praise and Glory of God.

> Rom 15:25-27 "25 Now, however, I am on my way to Jerusalem in the service of the saints there. 26 For Macedonia and Achaia were pleased to make a contribution for the poor among the saints in Jerusalem. 27 They were pleased to do it, and indeed they owe it to them. For if the Gentiles have shared in the Jews' spiritual blessings, they owe it to the Jews to share with them their material blessings."

Now what the Church at Achaia did, we are able to do also. We can learn to excel in the grace of giving to the poor in the Kingdom of God by submitting to the gospel of Jesus Christ. Each of us should use whatever gifts we are given to serve one another faithfully according to the grace of God. Loving one another by helping one another is the power that unifies us and displays Christ to the world. Thank you God for your gift of Grace!

Ephesians 6:24

Grace be with all them

that love our Lord Jesus Christ

in sincerity.

Amen.

Love the Foundation of Giving

Love is the tie that binds all things together.

The abundant grace of God is poured out on all of us who love God sincerely. It is the love of God toward us that enables grace to flow on our behalf.

God is Love

There is one area in our life that absolutely must be pruned and cultivated to produce lasting fruit, otherwise all we do, all we say and all our good intentions mean nothing and will profit us nothing. This area is Love!

We can sell everything we have and give it to the poor and if it is not done in love we earn no reward.

1 Corinthians 13:3 "And if I give all my possessions to feed the poor... but do not have love, it profits me nothing."

When we give to the needy, is God's reward enough?

Our motivation for giving is not to be merely to receive rewards. Let me say that again, giving should not be done to receive rewards. I have spent a considerable amount of time teaching the rewards of giving according to the Word of God. Love must be our motivation for giving just as love is God's motivation for giving. For God so loved the world He gave, (John 3:16). It is with a foundation of love, God gives. God is Love. Therefore we are to give as God gives, out of a foundation of Love. Love is what God, the Lord of the harvest, responds to when He distributes rewards for giving. First things must be first in the Kingdom. Without love as the foundation of giving to our brothers and sisters in Christ our giving is like a worldly lottery system rooted in selfishness and focused on greed. In many churches in the 21st century, the reward of giving is emphasized void of the need to love as the foundation of giving. Because of this teaching many aren't seeing the rewards of giving on the earth because their foundation for giving is not built on love but on receiving material possessions and money in exchange for their sowing. Some teachers and preachers are promising houses, land, job promotions, businesses, bills paid off, you name it, and they claim it when they sow their seed. Now their focus is on receiving what they asked for and not on God's reward. Again, when you give to the needy is God's reward enough for you?

We can vow to give all of our money, half of our money or some of our money to the poor, it doesn't matter what we vow. We can give 100%, 50% or 15% of all our possessions to the poor, it doesn't matter what we give. If it's not done out of the Love of God working in us, it's just like sweeping trash under the carpet. We know we've swept, we feel the bumps under the carpet every time we walk on the carpet but the sweeping didn't profit us anything it just gave us a lumpy carpet. You might be saying well that's a silly analogy. The truth is at first I thought it was also and I couldn't understand why God gave it to me that way, until now. Giving without love is like walking on a bumpy carpet of trash. It's not good for anything especially not for its intended purpose. Trash is meant to go in the trash can and carpet is meant to be smooth and comfortable to walk on; but instead two unlikely unions are made, trash and carpet. The two together profits no one. Just like giving without love, these are two unlikely unions that profit the giver nothing. However, giving with Love goes together and they profit the giver both on earth and in heaven. Now we have discovered why people can't buy their way into heaven!

The love of God has been poured into our hearts by the Holy Spirit. This is the promised gift from our Father to all who believe on Him through Jesus Christ. There is no amount of giving to the poor whether $10, $10,000, $10,000,000 or all the money in the world that would bring us heavenly treasures without the perfect love of God working in us and overflowing out of us.

What does God mean by love?

Love is:

• patient

- kind

- not jealous

- not arrogant

- not provoked

Love does:

- not brag

- not act unbecomingly

- not seek its own

- not take into account a wrong suffered

- not rejoice in unrighteousness, but rejoices with the truth

Love totally:

- bears all things

- believes all things

- hopes all things

- endures all things

Love never fails (1 Corinthians 13:1-8)

Another word for love is charity. Thus charity never fails!

The love of God binds all acts of charity, forgiveness, kindness, compassion, patience, humility and gentleness together. When we forgive one another we love one another. When we are kind and compassionate to another we love them. When we are patient and gentle with someone we show them our love. When we humble ourselves we love. Love is the tie that binds all things together in perfect unity, like a ribbon ties around a bunch of flowers binding them together. God is love and His love unifies us together perfectly.

Col 3:12-14 Therefore, as God's chosen people, holy and dearly loved, clothe yourselves with compassion, kindness, humility, gentleness and patience. 13 Bear with each other and forgive whatever grievances you may have against one another. Forgive as the Lord forgave you. 14 And over all these virtues put on love, which binds them all together in perfect unity,

Love is the fruit of the Holy Spirit that works in us. Since we live by the Spirit, let us keep in step with the Spirit. (Galatians 5:22-25)

God commands us to Love one another.

John 13:34 "A new command I give you: Love one another. As I have loved you, so you must love one another.

How can we say we love God whom we don't see, but don't love our brethren who we do see? Anyone who does not love his brother cannot love God. God has given us this command: "Whoever loves God must also love his brother." (1 John 4:20-21)

The scriptures speak for themselves. We must love one another!

One of my Seminary professors, Dr. Craig S. Keener, embodied to me the love of God. He is a well read and well known author and scholar in the academic circles. What was honorable and note worthy of mentioning is that He gave the vast majority of his income to the poor and needy in Africa. He lives in a small apartment and wares very modest clothing. I asked him, why did he give so much of his income away? He answered in his normally soft voice and said "because they need it more than I do". Wow, what love for our brethren. He looked not only to his own needs but also to the needs of the poor, weak and needy.

Blessed be the name of the Lord for your children who share your love. Help us all to love one another.

Loving God is not an option for believers.

Jesus said that the greatest commandment is: The LORD our God is one, Love the Lord your God with all your heart, mind, soul and strength (Mark 12:29-30)

We must go beyond professing our love for God out of our mouths only to displaying our love for God outwardly by our actions. Doing what God says is showing our love for Him. There is no distinction between obedience to God's command and loving Him.

John 14:23 'Jesus replied, "If anyone loves me, he will obey my teaching. My Father will love him, and we will come to him and make our home with him.'

Amazing, loving God is not about feelings; it's about obedience to His commandments and His commands alone.

Loving our sisters and brothers in Christ is also not an option for believers.

Jesus continued saying, "the second commandment is like the first, love your neighbor as yourself." (Matthew 22:39-40)

God has something to say about loving our neighbors...

John 13:35 "By this all men will know that you are my disciples, if you love one another."

Romans 12:10 "Be devoted to one another in brotherly love. Honor one another above yourselves."

Romans 13:8 "Let no debt remain outstanding, except the continuing debt to love one another, for he who loves his fellowman has fulfilled the law."

Galatians 5:13 "You, my brothers, were called to be free. But do not use your freedom to indulge the sinful nature ; rather, serve one another in love."

Ephesians 4:2 "Be completely humble and gentle; be patient, bearing with one another in love."

Hebrews 10:24 "And let us consider how we may spur one another on toward love and good deeds."

1 John 4:7 "Dear friends, let us love one another, for love comes from God. Everyone who loves has been born of God and knows God."

1 John 4:11 "Dear friends, since God so loved us, we also ought to love one another."

1 John 4:12 "No one has ever seen God; but if we love one another, God lives in us and his love is made complete in us."

The greatest of all spiritual acts is Love.

1 Corinthians 13:13 "Now Faith, Hope and Love abide, but the greatest of these is Love"

We should not neglect to love. (Luke 11:42) Our foundation is Love because God who is Love dwells in us. Therefore we are love, conformed to God's image. Who we are should be displayed out of us. They shall know us by our fruit. When we love, the good fruit of God (the fruit of the Spirit) is displayed out of us.

> Rom 12:9-13 "9 Love must be sincere. Hate what is evil; cling to what is good. 10 Be devoted to one another in brotherly love. Honor one another above yourselves. 11 Never be lacking in zeal, but keep your spiritual fervor, serving the Lord. 12 Be joyful in hope, patient in affliction, faithful in prayer. 13 Share with God's people who are in need."

Our giving should be motivated by our love for God. Our obedience to God's word on giving to the poor will prove our love for God and our love for our neighbor.

It is love that saves. Love helps, hopes, and operates in faith. It is love that shows mercy and grace. Love gives and is unselfish. Love provides for the needs of others. Love is the greatest gift of all. Don't let the moments to share God's love pass you by. Seek to love above all things; seek to love God and seek to love your neighbors. Bless the world with your love.

It is God's love in us that positions us to receive His indescribable gift of grace and positions us to excel in God's grace of giving.

1 Corinthians 3:6-9

6 I planted the seed, Apollos watered it, but God made it grow.

7 So neither he who plants nor he who waters is anything, but

only God, who makes things grow.

8 The man who plants and the man who waters

have one purpose, and each will be rewarded

according to his own labor.

9 For we are God's fellow workers;

you are God's field, God's building.

Preparing for the Rain

Preparing for your future.

Prepare your field.

Plant your seed.

Water the ground.

And watch God make it grow.

Many people sow with their mind set on the present time. Today I need or by tomorrow I have to have and because of my present need I will sow today to reap now. This is an incorrect view of sowing. Sowing prepares us for the future and the eternal. There is a process to sowing that starts with preparing our fields to receive the seed. The next step is waiting for the rain or watering the field and then watching the seed grow. Sowing the seed is in the beginning of the reaping process that produces at the end of this process, our future harvest.

Are you prepared for the future? Do you want your future to look different than your present?

Jesus' messages were to prepare us for the future. The message of repentance was to prepare His creation to receive of the Kingdom of God. (Matthew 4:17) The message of, 'be always on watch and pray', was to prepare us for the Day of Judgment so that we will be able to stand before the Son of God. (Luke 21:36) Here are a few more examples of Jesus' teachings telling us to be prepared for the future.

The Parable of the Unjust Steward – Luke 16:1-15

The unjust steward was dishonest, but he was still commended for his shrewd business practice in dealing with the people of this world who could help him in the future to care for his needs and welcome him into their houses. God is teaching us as His disciples of light, to also prepare for the future by using our wealth to help our own kind, other disciples of the light. We are considered trustworthy in handling wealth when we first help our brothers and sisters of the light by forgiving their debts and/or having mercy on their needs. As a result we too prepare for the future by gaining friends and when the worldly wealth is gone we will be welcomed into eternal dwellings. Investing in the lives of other disciples proves we are ready to receive true riches found only in Christ Jesus our Lord. Everyone who is found trustworthy with a little will be trusted with much but whoever is not trustworthy with a little will not be trusted to receive the promised riches of Jesus' Kingdom. Jesus said, in Luke chapter 16 verses 8-12, 8 "The master commended the dishonest manager because he had acted shrewdly. For the people of this world are more shrewd in dealing with their own kind than are the people of the light. 9 I tell you, use worldly wealth to gain friends for yourselves, so that when it is gone, you will be welcomed into eternal dwellings. 10 "Whoever can be trusted with very little can also be trusted with much, and whoever is dishonest with very little will also be dishonest with much. 11 So if you have not been trustworthy in handling worldly wealth, who will trust you with true riches?"

The Parable of the Ten Virgins – Matthew 25:1-13

Five virgins prepared for the future and five others did not. All ten virgins took their lamps but only five took extra oil for their lamps. God calls a lamp His word or commandment. (Psalms 119:105, Proverbs 6:23) Those who took additional oil with them were prepared for the future ensuring their lamps would always be full of light. Those who did not bring more oil did not prepare for the future but only looked at the present need for oil. Eventually their oil ran out putting out their light. The five virgins with the continuously lighted lamps represent the righteous and the five virgins whose lamp was put out represent the wicked. Proverbs 13:9 "The light of the righteous shines brightly, but the lamp of the wicked is snuffed out."

The wicked did not properly prepare for the coming of the bridegroom even though they had the word of God (the lamp). They did not obey God's word and therefore were not prepared for the bridegroom's future coming. On the other hand the five righteous virgins were ready for the bridegrooms coming when the door was open for them. They kept God's covenant and obeyed His word was prepared for the future coming of the bridegroom.

Psalm 132:12, 17 "12 If thy children will keep my covenant and my testimony that I shall teach them, their children shall also sit upon thy throne for evermore. 17 There will I make the horn of David to bud: I have ordained a lamp for mine anointed."

God has ordained a lamp for his anointed and that lamp prepares us for the future coming of Jesus Christ. "Therefore keep watch, because you do not know the day or the hour". (Matthew 25:13)

The Parable of the Sower – Luke 8:4-15

The farmer sowed the seed of the Word of God along the path, on the rock, among thorns and on good soil. The seed on good soil stands for those with a noble and good heart, who heard the word (the seed sown into the heart), retained it, and who persevered in the word of God producing a future crop. However, those who heard the word but did not receive it retain it and persevere in it because either:

- Satan snatched it from their hearts causing them not to believe,

- Temptation turned them away from what their hearts initially received with joy and believed for only a little while

- Life's worries, pleasures or riches choked the word of God they believed in out of their heart causing them not to mature in the Word

The result for those who heard the word who were on the path, the rock or among thorns is they were not able to produce a crop. The word of God is the only seed sown that produces a future crop that last.

The word of God, the seed sown in you, produces an action of seed sowing by you into the lives of God's people. Our seed sown is a direct reflection of God's seed first sown and rooted in us. It has been given to us to know, recognize and understand the mysteries and secrets of the Kingdom of God. (Luke 8:9) Once we hear the mysteries and secrets of sowing and reaping in the Kingdom of God, and we persevere and operate in the knowledge of this truth then we will be successful and prosperous in reaping a harvest as much as 100 times more than was sown.

Seed sowing is about the future. It is not about the past or the present. What we do in the present directly impact and reflects what we receive in the near and far future. Our present actions prepare us for our future provision and rewards. Prepare the field of your heart to receive, retain the word and persevere to maturity in the word of God making yourself ready for the rain that's coming to produce your harvest. There are those who prepare their fields and those who don't. There are those whose lamp always has light and those whose lamp's light is destined to be put out. There are those of the light who use their wealth wisely and shrewdly helping their own kind and those who don't. Which ones do you think is prepared when the rain comes? Prepare your field for the future rain and future harvest!

"He who has ears to hear, let him hear" (Luke 8:8)

2 Corinthians 9:15

Thanks be to God for his indescribable gift!

Grace the force of God that unifies us.

> Acts 20:32-35 "32 Now I commit you to God and to the word
> of his grace, which can build you up and give you an inheri-
> tance among all those who are sanctified. 33 I have not coveted
> anyone's silver or gold or clothing. 34 You yourselves know that
> these hands of mine have supplied my own needs and the needs
> of my companions. 35 In everything I did, I showed you that
> by this kind of hard work we must help the weak, remembering
> the words the Lord Jesus himself said: 'It is more blessed to give
> than to receive.'"

God spoke to me the following phrase one day when I was praying
about this book,

"As it began, so will it end."

As believers began the church sharing their possessions, having all
things in common and not counting anything as their own possession
any longer; so too shall we see this same love and selflessness among the
saints of God in Jesus Christ before the end.   Jesus has given us His
glory, full of grace and truth, to be one as Jesus and the Father is one;
one in thought, word and mission. It is by Jesus' glory we are bought
into complete unity. God will bring the church back to our first love
and our first works. Unified in the faith, being of one mind in Christ,
being made perfect in oneness, attaining to the full measure of Christ
is God's goal for us who believe.

Unity in the body of Christ

The manifested oneness of the body of Christ will only be attained
by displaying our love for one another openly and regularly. God's
next move in the body of Christ is Unity. The Love that we show to our
brothers and sisters accomplishes two spiritual missions:

1.   To let the world know absolutely Jesus is the sent son of God, the Messiah, the Savior of the World. Our Love for one another directs the attention of the world to the love of God for Jesus and for His disciples.

John 17:20-23 "20 My prayer is not for them alone. I pray also for those who will believe in me through their message, 21 that all of them may be one, Father, just as you are in me and I am in you. May they also be in us so that the world may believe that you have sent me. 22 I have given them the glory that you gave me, that they may be one as we are one: 23 I in them and you in me. May they be brought to complete unity to let the world know that you sent me and have loved them even as you have loved me."

2.   It will show Jesus Christ to those Jews who have rejected Him and whose heart has been hardened as a result of unbelief. The grace of Salvation that has come to the Gentiles who believe will provoke Israel to jealousy causing God's covenant chosen people to turn back to Him and be healed. They will know absolutely that Jesus is the sent son of God, the Messiah, their promised Savior.

Romans 11:7-12   "7 What then? What Israel sought so earnestly it did not obtain, but the elect did. The others were hardened, 8 as it is written: "God gave them a spirit of stupor, eyes so that they could not see and ears that they could not hear, to this very day." 9 And David says: "May their table become a snare and a trap, a stumbling block and a retribution for them. 10 May their eyes be darkened so they cannot see, and their backs be bent forever." 11 Again I ask: Did they stumble so as to fall beyond recovery? Not at all! Rather, because of their transgression, salvation has come to the Gentiles to make Israel envious. 12 But if their transgression means riches for the world, and their loss means riches for the Gentiles, how much greater riches will their fullness bring!"

God has a method to His plan.

When God makes a covenant with His people He is bound to it and never breaks it. (Judges 2:1)

I want to challenge you today to believe God with all your heart, mind, soul and strength, that you are more blessed when you are giving then you could ever be when you are receiving. Our giving ensures our future receiving on earth and in heaven; temporal and eternal harvest come to us when we give according to the Word of God. The faith-wealth of the Kingdom of God is in the hands of the children of God; our hands!

Our greatest blessing occurs when we give to brothers and sisters of Jesus Christ our Lord because in turn we are blessing Him. Jesus is the seed of Abraham's covenant. Those in Christ are of Abraham's seed and those who bless the seed of Abraham will be blessed. It is through Christ Jesus all the nations of the earth will be blessed.

Genesis 12:3 "I will bless those who bless you, "

Do the faith-works of the LORD helping those less fortunate. Open your eyes, open your heart, use your hands, legs and skill to up-lift, build up, supply the need of, encourage, feed, clothe, give shelter to, disciple and help those in need. Don't neglect your covenant brothers and sisters in Christ and your natural born family. Display Christ on the earth. Use the glory Jesus left with us to do the work that He did on earth and even greater works because He sits at the right hand of our Father in Heaven. (John 17:21-23, John 14:12, Mark 16:19) The right hand of God is not a seat it's a position of honor, power and authority. The right hand of God is the power of God. Jesus left us a legacy of glory to fulfill our destiny predetermined by Him.

Bless the LORD our God by loving Him and loving those whom He loves. For this is the greatest commandment of all:

Mark 12:28-31 "...Of all the commandments, which is the most important? 29 "The most important one," answered Jesus, "is this: 'Hear, O Israel, the Lord our God, the Lord is one. 30 Love the Lord your God with all your heart and with all your soul and with all your mind and with all your strength.' 31 The second is this: 'Love your neighbor as yourself.' There is no commandment greater than these."

In reality, many who want to love their neighbor by giving to supply their needs don't have the overflow enough to generously give. They wonder how they can give when they can't squeeze another dime out of their paycheck. Sometimes they don't earn enough income. Other times they do make enough but they spent over what their daily expenses require. Mortgage payments, credit card debt, car loans, medical bills, and many other expenses owed above their income are their bondage. Thus establishing a lifestyle of giving to those we owe to the neglect of establishing a lifestyle of giving to God and to those in need. These are bound to the lender leaving them without the freedom to give or lend generously.

The heart of a man makes his plans but it is God who orders his steps. (Proverbs 16:9) The choice between serving money and possessions and serving God may be a difficult choice for some believers but let us consider our ways and turn our steps toward God's teaching and instructions. When we allow God to speak to us, He changes us from the inside out. God wants us to be generous givers and he wants us to live abundantly. Giving and Abundant living through grace filled sowing and reaping go hand in hand in the Kingdom of God. As a result of obedience to God's Word, He promises we will live in multiplied grace where God is able to make all grace abound toward us; always having all sufficiency in all things and always abounding in every good work: (2 Corinthians 9:8) Take your rightful place in the Kingdom of God and excel in the grace of giving. God wants us to be ruler over much as we are proven to be faithful over a little. Never despise small beginnings for this is where we will be tested and this is from where we will be exalted by God.

Every believer will be tested in the area of money and possessions. We have to prove we love God and we do not love money or possessions. Money is not the root of all evil but the love of money is!

During the testing period(s) the devil will try to convince us God didn't really mean we'd have to give tithes, appointed times offerings and alms offerings to support the weak, poor and needy. The devil will try to convince us God didn't really mean we would be more blessed when we give than when we receive especially during harder times. By the influence of Satan some will most likely try to reason away God's instruction to give and instead hold on to what they have accumulated. For those who love God more than money, they will listen to the Holy Spirit and allow Him to sanctify them in the truth. Once we are sanctified by the truth, we will pass the test of God proving our love for God by being obedient to His call to give and help others as we are able. For others, they will fail this test. They will hold on to their money and possessions. They will not let them go and especially not something they feel is valuable or sentimental to them proving to God that their possessions and money is their god. For those who have failed this test in the past or who find themselves failing today or in the future, repentance is still a valid option. Repent of your sin and turn from loving money and possessions to loving God more than any thing. There is no more condemnation for those who are in Christ Jesus because in Christ the law of the Spirit of Life has set us free from the law of sin and death. (Romans 8:1-4) So get up and start over again. God loves us and wants us to pass the test. Use God's grace – our enabler that strengthens us and provides us with everything we need to pass the test.

In order to pass the test we need to truly walk with God allowing Him to teach, correct and chastise us when necessary; allowing Him to show us our faults in the mirror and allow God to love us greater than anyone else has or could through this mind transformation. Surrendering our will, our wants and desires, our goals and dreams and our life to GOD will show us whom we choose the god of mammon (money) or our Father God in Heaven. This is the cost of being a disciple of Jesus Christ, to lay down our lives and bear our cross daily. (Luke 14:26, 27, 33) No one can serve two masters, we will love the one and hate the other or we will be devoted to one and despise the other. No one can serve both God and money. (Luke 16:13)

As I am completing the writing of this book, the United States of America is experiencing, as some have said, its biggest financial crisis since "The Great Depression". Many are seeing their wealth made or stored in the financial markets decline sharply. Jobs are being lost, credit is being frozen, some are loosing their homes to foreclosure and general fear is pervasive even among believers in Jesus Christ. I want to take this time to encourage the citizens of Heaven in Christ Jesus. My hope is the words that I have written will strengthen the resolve of the citizens of the commonwealth of Israel. God is God. He is our faithful God who promises to keep His covenant of love to those who love Him and keep His commands to a thousand generations. (Deuteronomy 7:9) Our generation is apart of God's great Kingdom economy. God is our source and He unites us by His glory, which is full of grace and truth. The commonwealth system of the Kingdom of God will provide for all who are in need. For it is certain God's children shall rise up with unselfish attitudes to redistribute God's faith-wealth according to God's will. Take comfort in knowing the voice of God is loud and clear. When we obey His voice, there will be no poor among our brothers and sisters in Christ just as God desires. (Deuteronomy 15:4-5) We are reminded we have all things in common under the head of the church, Jesus Christ our LORD. The wealth of God's Kingdom is provided to all through all.

During hard economic times there will be more poor among us and God is calling us to help lift up our brothers and sisters in Christ. Are we listening?

As followers of Jesus Christ we should be careful not to let the cares, lust and passions of this world turn us away from doing what's right in the sight of God. Believers our God is our judge and guide. God's grace will enable us to love one another as we love ourselves. He unifies us through our giving and receiving, our sowing and reaping when we sow what God has placed in our hands. Fellow citizens of heaven let us not love wealth. Let us resign ourselves to using wealth for the good purpose of God to supply the needs of all His people and grow the Kingdom of God.

We all have been given a voice to communicate what we believe personally and corporately about finances and material possessions and how to and how not to use them. Free will can be exercised and our beliefs should be expressed about giving. As a result, there are many voices we hear day to day and some we are influenced by. Above all the voices that are articulated throughout the world, the voice of God is the one that should be respected, honored and obeyed. What God has to say should be the highest and most important persuasion that guides our actions. In this way we show that we are "...not ashamed of the gospel of Jesus Christ which is the power of God for salvation of everyone who believes: first for the Jew then for the Gentile. For in the gospel righteousness from God is revealed, a righteousness that is by faith from first to last, just as it is written: "The righteous will live by faith." (Romans 1:16-17) Our righteous response is faith in God. Read His word and listen to the Holy Spirit and we will always find that God has something to say about that...

Now my fellow believers in God through Jesus Christ our Lord, I commend you to God and to the word of his grace which is able to build you up and to give you an inheritance among all them which are sanctified in the truth. Give ear to what the Spirit of the Lord is saying. We ought to support the weak and remember the words of Jesus Christ, "It is more blessed to give than to receive" (Acts 20: 32, 35)

It is God's grace that enables all of us to achieve the works God has predestined for us to do before the world began. (Ephesians 2:10)

Thank you God, for your Indescribable Gift of Grace!

Now to the King eternal, immortal, invisible, the only God, be honor and glory for ever and ever. Amen. (1Timothy 1:17)

Isaiah 58:8-11

8 Then your light will break forth like the dawn,

and your healing will quickly appear;

then your righteousness will go before you,

and the glory of the LORD will be your rear guard.

9 Then you will call, and the LORD will answer;

you will cry for help, and he will say: Here am I.

"If you do away with the yoke of oppression,

with the pointing finger and malicious talk,

10 and if you spend yourselves in behalf of the hungry

and satisfy the needs of the oppressed,

then your light will rise in the darkness,

and your night will become like the noonday.

11 The LORD will guide you always;

he will satisfy your needs in a sun-scorched land

and will strengthen your frame.

You will be like a well-watered garden,

like a spring whose waters never fail.

Appendix: Money

We love God and we desire to do what pleases Him. We are not always sure of what does please Him, especially in the area of money. We are sure God wants us to provide for our families and bring our tithes, give our offerings and now we know with confidence we should also use our money to contribute generously to the needs of the poor and needy. But what else does God expect us to do with our money?

God expects us to leave an Inheritance for our children.

Proverbs 13:22 "A good man leaves an inheritance for his children's children, but a sinner's wealth is stored up for the righteous."

God expects use to use the wealth we obtain in the world to gain friends – to love and be merciful with our own kind, the people of the light in Jesus Christ.

Luke 16:9 "I tell you, use worldly wealth to gain friends for yourselves, so that when it is gone, you will be welcomed into eternal dwellings."

God expects us to have investments- to make a profit on our faith-wealth.

Matthew 25:27 "Well then, you should have put my money on deposit with the bankers, so that when I returned I would have received it back with interest."

God expects us to pay our debts to our debtors.

> Ezekiel 18:5, 7 "5 But if a man be just, and do that which is lawful and right, 7And hath not oppressed any, but hath restored to the debtor his pledge, hath spoiled none by violence, hath given his bread to the hungry, and hath covered the naked with a garment;"

God expects us to use Integrity and Honesty in our oversight and use of money in our businesses and professions.

Luke 16:10-12   "10Whoever can be trusted with very little can also be trusted with much, and whoever is dishonest with very little will also be dishonest with much. 11 So if you have not been trustworthy in handling worldly wealth, who will trust you with true riches? 12 And if you have not been trustworthy with someone else's property, who will give you property of your own?"

God also has expectations for us in what not to do to make money or what not to do in the use of our money.

God expects us not to make money on the backs of the poor.

- Don't oppress the poor to increase your wealth and don't give gifts to the rich.

Proverbs 22:16 "He who oppresses the poor to increase his wealth and he who gives gifts to the rich—both come to poverty."

- Do not charge exorbitant interest on loans.

Proverbs 28:8 "He who increases his wealth by exorbitant interest amasses it for another, who will be kind to the poor."

Money is made by man from wood and metal

Money has no ears it cannot hear.

Money has no eyes it can not see.

Money has no hands or feet, it can not move on its own.

Money has no mind it can neither think or reason nor judge or reveal.

Money doesn't provide wisdom, knowledge, counsel or understanding.

Money doesn't know right from wrong.

Money doesn't make your life easy or burden free

Money doesn't make us somebody

As a man thinks, so he is

Money cannot define us

Money cannot represent us

Money cannot bring us peace, joy or happiness

Money cannot make us

Money cannot break us

Money cannot bring us love

Money can only do what our heart, mind, soul or spirit directs it to do. What we think about money will determine what we do with it. We can either be wise or foolish with money. The foolish see money as their shelter. The foolish see money as their problem solver, decision maker or guide thus giving money power that it doesn't have. They give money a high place in their lives causing money to become their "god". The foolish love and trust money to such an extent they believe it can save them, provide for them, create for them, protect them and bring them power, strength and glory. The Bible says, fools have no desire to get wisdom so what good is money in their hands? (Proverbs 17:16)

The wise have wisdom for their shelter and some people have money as their shelter. The difference between these two shelters is wisdom has the advantage in preserving your life.

Ecclesiastes 7:11-12 "11 Wisdom, like an inheritance, is a good thing and benefits those who see the sun. 12 Wisdom is a shelter as money is a shelter, but the advantage of knowledge is this: that wisdom preserves the life of its possessor."

Money in the hands of the wise can be the answer to all things. (Ecclesiastes 10:19) Money in the hands of fools brings no good. (Proverbs 17:16) Godly wisdom in using money can answer the call to overcome poverty, mental and physical sicknesses, homelessness, malnutrition, religious persecution, enslavement, debt, famine, suffering, nakedness, oppression and more. Money in the hands of the holy is willingly shared to help support church leaders, the weak, the poor and needy, friends and family in need, godly ministries, to pay taxes, to provide resources for godly projects and buildings and so on. Wisdom reveals we are not to put our hope in money which is so uncertain but we are to put our hope in God who richly provides us with everything, including money for our enjoyment. (1 Timothy 6:17, emphasis mine)

1 Timothy 6:18-19 "18 Command them to do good, to be rich in good deeds, and to be generous and willing to share. 19 In this way they will lay up treasure for themselves as a firm foundation for the coming age, so that they may take hold of the life that is truly life."

Money is not evil

But the love of money is the root of all kinds of evil

No one can have two gods; we will hate one and love the other

Anyone who loves money can not love God

Anyone who loves money has made money their god

Ecclesiastes 5:10 "Whoever loves money never has money enough; whoever loves wealth is never satisfied with his income. This too is meaningless."

Money is not to be served

Money is not to be treasured or hoarded

Money is not to be admired

Money is temporal and not eternal

Money can be lost, stolen or misused

Money without God's wisdom is not the answer to all things

Ecclesiastes 5:13-15 "13 I have seen a grievous evil under the sun: wealth hoarded to the harm of its owner, 14 or wealth lost through some misfortune, so that when he has a son there is nothing left for him. 15 Naked a man comes from his mother's womb, and as he comes, so he departs. He takes nothing from his labor that he can carry in his hand."

Money is a gift from God

We should use it to serve God and to serve our neighbor.

About the Author

Danielle Martin Moffett is the loving wife of Frank Jr. and the mother of four beautiful children, Jade, Jordan, Frank 3rd and Daniel. She is the visionary and Administrator of Arising Ministries. Arising Ministries' mission is to generously supply the needs of God's people who are poor materially, financially and spiritually in Jerusalem and in all parts of the world. She is a prophetess of God with the accurate word of the Lord in her mouth. She is a woman of faith and has the heart to see the people of God walk in greatness on every level.

After 20 years of experience in Corporate America as an Engineer and Information Technology Manager, God called Danielle out to full time service as a writer, teacher and preacher of His word. She is a graduate of the University of Delaware and she is completing her Masters of Theology Degree from Palmer Theological Seminary in Pennsylvania. She is a leader and active member at Personal Touch Christian Center in Newark, Delaware.

She is God's inspired teacher, preacher, speaker, writer and author. You are welcomed to contact Arising Ministries by email at **dmmoffett@netscape.net**.